The
Birth
of Your
Destiny

Victoria Boyson

The Birth of Your Destiny

To place orders, you may contact us at
Victoria Boyson, Inc.
P.O. Box 10441
Cedar Rapids, IA 52410
Phone: (319) 365-9570
Fax: (319) 365-9570
Email: info@boyson.org
Visit our website at www.boyson.org

Co-published with
Arrow Publications, Inc.
P.O. Box 10102
Cedar Rapids, IA 52410
Phone: (319) 395-7833
Toll Free: (877) 363-6889 (U.S. only)
Fax: (319) 395-7353
Arrow Publications website: www.arrowbookstore.com

This book is dedicated with gratitude to my mother,
Ellen Mae Friedrich.

Although, I had her for no more than sixteen years,
in that short time she prepared me for life
by introducing me to her best friend Jesus.

She was and is a great lady!

CONTENTS

FOREWORD

I have known Victoria Boyson for many years. During these years she and her husband Steve have faithfully served both on my staff and in ministry at our church. Throughout this time, Victoria has consistently positioned herself to be an encouragement to all who know her.

Indeed, in our world, with all that assaults our spirits, with the effects of our battles and our bruises, we need those who are anointed to help us win our battles and reach our goals. We also need the wisdom that is found in these pages: how to understand not only the delays of the enemy, but also the delays of God. Truly, the release of our destiny is intimately intertwined with our knowledge of the ways of God.

The Birth of Your Destiny not only instructs you about theological facts pertaining to destiny, but the fact that this book is in your hands tells me that you are well on your way to the fulfillment of your destiny. It will provide important keys to unlocking the fullness of God's plan for your life.

Francis Frangipane

A special thanks to . . .

Thank you to my incredibly gifted husband, Steve, without whose help this book would never have been written. Thank you for all of your encouraging pushing and praying. I love you.

Thank you to Mom and Dad Boyson and a special thank you to my children, Cassandra, Cody, Cole and Cailie-Ellen. Thank you for all your prayers!

Thank you all very much,

Victoria

INTRODUCTION

*W*hen my youngest child Cailie-Ellen was about seven weeks old, she became very fussy, as all newborns do at times. My husband and I tried everything to calm her, but to no avail. As I rocked her, I determined in my heart to listen to the voice of the Lord for His guidance in helping her. The Lord led me to put her in her swing, but it did not help. Then He led me to turn on the vacuum, it helped for a short while and then she began to cry again. We felt led to massage her, but again it brought her only temporary relief. Then finally again I felt led to rock her and she soon fell fast asleep.

A bit confused, I questioned the Lord, "Did I miss your leading previously?" since it seemed as though nothing I felt led to do helped her except what I was doing to begin with. The Lord spoke to me that I did not miss His leading, *"but every step was necessary."*

Later the Lord brought back this memory to me. It was then that I realized the premise of what God was speaking —that the promise of our destiny is an unfolding process and each step is important to its fulfillment. Fulfilling our destiny is a journey, and each step of that journey is important.

So often when God speaks a word into our hearts we expect to see the desired results right after doing what He has asked us to do. We get despondent when we do not see things happen right away. But we need to understand this concept: *everything we go through, even our failures, is important to the fulfillment of the promise He has given us.* Every step is necessary! There may have been an easier or shorter way, but He is saying everything we go through is important, it has a purpose.

So it is when we give birth in the natural realm to a baby. We cannot expect to give birth the day after the doctor tells us we are expecting a child. The baby must go through stages of development in order to be healthy. Each stage in the baby's development is important; nothing that we experience during this period is unnecessary, but each step has a purpose. We never look at a newly pregnant woman and judge her fruit by the way she looks on the outside. We trust that in time she will begin to show and we will see that she will indeed bear a child.

We must begin to see each other prophetically and not judge by what *our* eyes see. God does not judge us moment by moment, but He looks at our lives from beginning to end. That is why He was able to refer to Gideon as a "mighty warrior" in Judges 6:12, before he had done even a single act of bravery. So it is with us, the day we are born God sees our entire life. He sees the outcome of every trial we face. Because of this, He pushes us on, encourages us and persuades us that going through the trial will be worth it. He encourages us that it is necessary, it is important.

Enter into this book with an open heart, ready to receive God's best for your life. Get ready to find JOY in the BIRTH OF YOUR DESTINY!

God is Looking for You

~ Chapter One ~

DON'T STOP NOW!

Giving birth to your destiny is a messy and exhausting process, but inevitably your misery will turn into joy and you will produce the product of grace that you have always dreamed of. You are much too close to the end to give up now. How do I know that? You have this book in your hands. God gave this book to you and He would not give it to just anyone, only to those who are ready to receive it.

Misery Turned to Joy

"O Lord, the king rejoices in your strength. How great is his joy in the victories you give! You have granted him the desire of his heart, and have not withheld the request of his lips" (Psalm 21:1–2). "For the king trusts in the Lord; through the unfailing love of the Most High he will not be shaken" (Psalm 21:7).

A s I read the above verses, the joy and praise David gave to our Lord touched me. He thanked God for the great blessings He had given him. God has answered his prayers and given him the desires of his heart.

The thankful praise that burst forth from David's heart seems a million miles away from the psalms he wrote in the midst of his trial. In the middle of his tribulation, he wrote psalms that expressed his misery and pain. He questioned if God were even with him (see Psalm 22:1). He groaned because he did not see the Lord answering his prayers (see Psalm 22:2). His misery was great, like that of a pregnant woman in the midst of labor.

In the midst of her labor she feels as though she cannot last; as though her pain is too great to bear. She does not care what anyone else thinks. She is in misery. But moments after it is all over and she has that beautiful baby in her hands, she begins to lose sight of her pain. She feels much like David did in Psalm 21:1 when he said, *"The king rejoices in your strength. How great is his joy in the victories you give!"* Her joy overshadows her hours of grief and the great pain she felt pales in comparison to the exuberant joy and peace she now feels.

Cailie-Ellen is Born

When my fourth child was born, I went through a terrible ordeal. I had delivered three other children before her and none of them were easy deliveries. But they failed to compare to the extraordinary pain I had when giving birth to her. For hours they induced my labor mercilessly until all I could do was cry. I did not care who saw me, nor did I care what they thought. I was in agonizing pain and, indeed, she was finally taken by caesarian section. I remember very little of being taken into surgery, but I do remember there were people all around me. I am not one who likes to let others see me cry, but at that moment I did not care. I bawled.

However, even with all the pain I had, I can say that it did not compare to the joy I had when the doctor announced, "It's a girl!" I had been given the desire of my heart and, at that moment, my trial had been *rendered powerless*. I felt as David felt when he said, *"You have granted him the desire of his heart and have not withheld the request of his lips" (Psalm 21:2).*

None of the pain I had endured mattered because God had answered my prayer. Cailie-Ellen Shirley was born. She was beautiful, healthy and perfect. She was the one bright spot during a very dark time in my life. God was faithful to me and I could say as David did, *"Through the victories you gave, his glory is great; you have bestowed on him splendor and majesty" (Psalm 21:5).*

Turn Your Misery Into Praise

As the Lord fulfills our destiny in Him and the promises He has made to us, the pain we felt during the trials we have faced will fade away into glorious praises. As a woman in labor knows her pain will produce a baby, *we have the knowledge that our pain will produce the promise of the Lord.* We *will* give birth to our destiny.

David sings a song of mourning and grief in Psalm 22, yet in the midst of his trial and pain he praises God: *"Yet, you are enthroned as the Holy One; you are the praise of Israel. In you our fathers put their trust; they trusted and you delivered them. They cried to you and were saved; in you they trusted and were not disappointed" (vv 3–5).*

David reminded himself that his forefathers had trusted in God and were not disappointed. He praised God for His faithfulness, even in the midst of his misery. There is a certain misery in trusting God even when the waves of doubt flood through your soul. However, we *"must believe and not doubt, because he who doubts is like a wave of the sea, blown and tossed by the wind" (James 1:6).* We must not doubt and let go of the promise of our destiny in Him. We must stay on course and not be turned to the right or left. The trying of our faith in Him will produce endurance—strength that we will need later on in life. *With every battle we endure, we grow stronger in Him.*

There are times when we, like David, cannot hear the voice of our God (see Psalm 22:2). He seems to be silent and we wonder if He still intends to fulfill the promise He has made to us. These are critical moments when our trust in Him is indeed tested—when doubts begin to pelt us like hailstones. Should we retreat like the double-minded man in James 1:8 and change course, or should we proceed, trusting in our God? We must stay on course! We must trust in Him! *We must not change our direction from the last instructions we have received from Him.* We know that trials will come, but *"Blessed is the man who perseveres under trial, because when he has stood the test he will receive" (James 1:12)* the promise.

Beloved, keep on believing . . . keep on trusting! Stay on course and surely, as an expectant mother, your pain will produce the promise. Keep trusting . . . keep praising Him, whether you feel like it or not. *The richest gift you can give to your heavenly Father is to praise Him in the midst of your pain.* Trust Him when you cannot see an answer, because *"every good and perfect gift is from above, coming down from the Father of the heavenly lights, who does not change" (James 1:17).*

The pain you now feel will be transformed into the sweetest of praises to our God. Your sorrow will be turned into joy. *"Through the unfailing love of the Most High he will not be shaken" (Psalm 21:7).* He will turn your mourning into dancing, and the rejection you have experienced into strength, through trusting in God. David experienced this, and you will, too!

Pray this with me:

Dear Father,
Open my eyes and my heart to receive vision and passion from this book, so that I may receive grace from heaven to press on through this journey and find my destiny in You.

~ Chapter Two ~

THE CONCEPTION
OF A DREAM

God wants to give you a dream for your future and implant the seeds of destiny in your heart. " 'I know the plans I have for you,' declares the Lord" (Jeremiah 29:11).

One day while praying, the Holy Spirit came upon me and I was overwhelmed with desperation to see the call of God fulfilled in my life. I cried out to God and asked Him to *do whatever He needed to do to me in order for the call of ministry on my life to be fulfilled.* I had no idea then how that prayer would change my life. The Lord began to reshape my life almost immediately.

What seemed then like the destruction of my ministry was really its redirection and explosion. God wasted no time in reforming every aspect of my life; not much of who I was remained. This was not an easy time for me, especially at the beginning when I did not quite understand what God was doing.

During this time the Lord gave me a promise: *"The Lord had said to Abram, 'Leave your country, your people and your father's household and go to the land I will show you. I will make you into a great nation and I will bless you; I will make your name great and you will be a blessing. I will bless those who bless you and whoever curses you I will curse; and all peoples on the earth will be blessed through you' "* (Genesis 12:1–3).

Very often in Scripture, we see God asking His people to make great sacrifices to accomplish His will in their lives. He shows us His plan for us so that we will be encouraged to endure to the end. Abraham did not immediately receive all that God had promised him upon leaving Haran. No, he went through many years of tedious waiting before the promise was fulfilled.

Reflecting God's Glory

Diamonds do not start out clean and brilliant; they are rather dull and full of flaws. Each stone must endure the long and tedious process of being cut, faceted and polished. They are carefully cut to remove flaws and to better reflect light. The art of stone cutting cannot be hurried or you risk damaging the precious gemstone, and it would then be of little value to anyone. After a diamond has gone through the cutting process it is one of the most desirable jewels on earth, with beauty and endurance unmatched.

If, for some reason, the cutter were to quit cutting only halfway through, the diamond would remain relatively worthless. The job must be completed. There are many different tools a cutter will use to cut and polish each stone to achieve the desired results. Likewise, God too uses many different *tools* to shape and perfect us—to make us who He needs us to become. There are many different tools God will use to cut, sand and polish each of us to achieve *His* desired goal.

God will use whatever He has to in order to accomplish His plan for our lives, but when He is done we are His masterpiece and we reflect His glory like diamonds reflect the light. He may remove things or people from our lives. He uses irritating people and circumstances to sand us down in areas of our lives, while He polishes us with His love. He takes His time and molds us into vessels He can use.

Holding His Light

"Make a lampstand of pure gold and hammer it out, base and shaft; its flowerlike cups, buds and blossoms shall be of one piece with it" (Exodus 25:31).

The Lord spoke to Moses on every aspect of the tabernacle, including the lampstands that would hold the fire that would light the tabernacle. God spent a great deal of time on the lampstands, taking great care to explain exactly how they were to be fashioned. He wanted them made of pure gold that was *hammered* out into the different designs.

The Lord has been working on His church with this same process of refining and, yes, even hammering us. He has put a great deal of time and thought into what He desires His church to look like. We are all different parts of the lampstand, but working together we will hold His glorious light.

"Arise, shine, for your light has come, and the glory of the Lord rises upon you. See, darkness covers the earth and thick darkness is over the peoples, but the Lord rises upon you and his glory appears over you. Nations will come to your light, and kings to the brightness of your dawn" (Isaiah 60:1–3).

Nations will come to our light as His glory will appear over us, but first we must be fashioned into His image. We must leave our place of comfort and step out into the unknown, following God at every step. He alone can direct us, but He is using the circumstances we are in to refine us. The more refining He does to us, the more radiantly His light will shine through us.

Fearfully and Wonderfully Made

The natural creation of a human being is a miraculous process. When God creates a child in the womb, He is like a diamond cutter or a goldsmith, using great care to add specific details to make them His stunning masterpiece. David said in Psalm 139:14, "I am fearfully and wonderfully made." God has designed you, too. Down to the last detail He crafted you, from the dimple on your chin to the freckles on your nose. He loves His creation.

Although the birth process is miraculous and wonderful, it is not always easy. It can be painful, exhausting and humiliatingly messy. The process, however tedious, does not detract from the wonder of the miracle of birth. And even the mess is an important and inevitable part of the process. We expect it to be hard work and we accept that as a part of the process. Then when we hold that precious little life in our hands, all the pain is swept away and joy takes its place.

If God would so meticulously create you at your birth, you can understand then that the birth of your destiny is equally important to Him. He is interested in its fulfillment down to the last detail. He forms us and refines us and then produces the fulfillment of the promise He has made to us. All we need to do is to trust Him and surrender to the process. In the end, we give birth to something perfectly suited to us.

Many times God has had to remind me to stay on His potter's wheel and abandon myself to His work in my life. I look back now and think, "How did God do that?" He took this lump of nothing and made a glorious reflection of His grace.

Left the way God found us, we would be unable to walk out the various callings that God has placed on our lives. God's continual refinement of our lives can be painful and exhausting, but worth it. The Lord our God is faithful to keep His promises.

Pray this with me:

Dear Father,

Help me to submit to Your reformation of my heart and life. Do whatever it takes to make me usable for Your glory. Grant me grace to stay with You in the place You have positioned me, no matter how messy it gets.

~ Chapter Three ~

GOD IS LOOKING FOR YOU

You are the "perfect fit" for God's plan!

"I will put in the desert the cedar and the acacia, the myrtle and the olive. I will set pines in the wasteland, the fir and the cypress together, so that people may see and know, may consider and understand, that the hand of the Lord has done this, that the Holy One of Israel has created it" (Isaiah 41:19–20).

*G*od is looking for a desert, so He can create a forest. Do you feel like a barren desert? If you feel there are 100 reasons why God would never use you, then rejoice, because those are the same 100 reasons why He will use you. When God is looking for someone to change the world, He looks for the most unlikely candidate. He has to use someone . . . *why not you?*

When God began looking for someone in whom He could build a great nation, He saw Sarah and said, *"She is perfect"* *(Genesis 17:16).* Wait a minute! Sarah was old and barren; she'd had no children. How could God build a nation from such as she? It was impossible, right? BUT God looks at the impossible and sees a promise. Why did God select Sarah? It was her barrenness that drew Him to her. *It was the impossibility of her situation that made her the perfect candidate for a miracle from heaven.*

Are you living with an impossible situation? If you are, then rejoice, because you are a perfect candidate for a miracle from God. It is your need that has drawn Him to you. If God sees a mighty nation in your belly, then believe Him. He is able to perform it.

God Wants to Do More for You

One of my favorite fairy tales is the story of Cinderella. This story represents to me the heart of God. Cinderella lived with a stepmother who despised her, and her greatest dream was to be loved. She was not dreaming of being a princess—that was too much for her to even conceive of. Her reason for going to the ball was to find a man who would love her. God did not want to give her just any man, it was *His* desire to give her *the prince.* The man that every other eligible female was dreaming of and conniving to get, God had held in reserve for her. *"Now to him who is able to do immeasurably more than all we ask or imagine" (Ephesians 3:20).*

As princess she would be loved and admired by not just a man, but a nation. When God is looking for a princess, He goes to the scullery and sees in a servant girl the ability to rule a nation. If life has pressed you down, then you need to rejoice! If life has passed you by, then you need to rejoice! If you feel forgotten and unloved, then you need to rejoice! You are just the one God is looking for to change the world!

"Sing, o barren woman, you who never bore a child; burst into song, shout for joy, you who were never in labor; because more are the children of the desolate woman" (Isaiah 54:1). "Enlarge the place of your tent" (Isaiah 54:2), because God is looking for you.

Do Not Limit God

When I was in school, my favorite sport was basketball. My problem was that I was only 5'2" tall. Yet I became quite proficient at basketball because I refused to let my size dictate to me my ability to play the game. My coach used *me* as a positive example to the other girls. I was one of the smallest girls on the team, but I learned to be aggressive and go after the ball no matter how big the other girls were—much like Jael in Judges 4.

Jael was a woman who was at home in her tent while the men of Israel went out to fight the battle against Sisera, the commander of the Canaanite army. God had promised to deliver Sisera into the hands of Barak, the leader of the Israelite army. Because of Barak's unbelief, God delivered him instead into the hands of a woman. That woman was Jael. Jael was at home minding the house when Sisera arrived on foot to the door of her tent. She lured him into her tent to rest. *"But Jael, Heber's wife, picked up a tent peg and a hammer and*

went quietly to him while he lay fast asleep, exhausted.
She drove the peg through his temple into the ground, and
he died" (Judges 4:21).

Jael was probably the last one that Barak considered
would win the battle for Israel that day, but God chose her for
that very reason. God was sending us a message: We cannot
limit Him! He refuses to be put in a box! Tell Him He cannot
do something and that is just what He will do. Give Him a
desert and He will make a forest. Give Him a servant girl and
He will make her a princess. Give Him a housewife and He
will make her a warrior. Give Him your barrenness and He will
make for you a great nation. *"So that people may see and*
know, may consider and understand, that the Lord has
done this, the Holy One of Israel has created it" (Isaiah
41:20).

This is God's heart concerning us. He sees beyond our
weaknesses and sees a mighty warrior. He calls those things
that are not, as though they were. If you feel discarded by life,
then rejoice, because God is looking for you! You are a
perfect fit for His purpose.

In the story of Cinderella, after she runs away from the ball,
everyone is looking for her. The highest officials in the kingdom
were furiously searching for her. Who was she that the entire
kingdom would be looking for her? She was the perfect fit!
She was the only one who fit the glass slipper.

And God says to you today: "You are the only one who can fill the 'shoes' that I am preparing for you. You are what I am looking for. You are what I need."

The Shunammite Woman

In 2 Kings 4:8–37, Elisha lived in the home of a Shunammite woman, in a room she had prepared especially for him. Whenever he traveled through that area, he stayed at her home and she asked for nothing in return for the kindness she had given him. It was difficult for her to receive the blessing he wanted to give her. She had blessed the man of God and had asked for nothing in return, but *God desired to bless her anyway.* Elisha sought out her need and, finding she had no son, spoke life into her situation. Her heart was so tender; she could not receive the words he spoke to her. She could not bring herself to hope again. Her disappointment at having no son was a burden to her heart. She had learned to live with her pain, her husband was well advanced in years and he had given her no sons. It was a great pain to her, but she had learned to cope with her disappointment. Knowing how great her pain was she did not want to be disappointed again.

"About this time next year," Elisha said, "you will have a son in your arms." "No, my lord," she objected. "Don't mislead your servant, O man of God!" (2 Kings 4:16).

A heart so bruised, a pain so deep that she could not bear to hope again. The Shunammite woman knew that she would not be able to suffer another disappointment. This was an area of her heart that was still very raw. Her longing for a son was so great that she was unwilling to entrust her heart to anyone. Into this painful situation, God breathed the breath of life. He raised her hope from the dead and she bore a son (see 2 Kings 4:17).

God did for her what was above and beyond all she could ask or hope or even think (see Ephesians 3:20). He raised her hopes from the dead (see 2 Kings 4:36). God sought her out to give her a miracle; He is doing the same for you today!

Have you been discarded by life? Then rejoice, because God is looking for YOU! Say "yes" to Him today!

~ Chapter Four ~

HANNAH'S DESTINY

All Hannah wanted was a son, but God wanted a prophet for His people and a friend for Himself.

"There was a certain man from Ramathaim, a Zuphite from the hill country of Ephraim, whose name was Elkanah . . . He had two wives; one was called Hannah and the other Peninnah. Peninnah had children, but Hannah had none" (1 Samuel 1:1–2). "And because the Lord had closed her womb, her rival kept provoking her in order to irritate her" (1 Samuel 1:6).

The story of these two women is not an uncommon one. God often uses irritating people to draw us closer to Him and to push us toward our destiny. God will put people in our lives that have what we want (and are willing to torture us with it) in order that we might *seek Him* for the fulfillment of the promise He has made to us.

Peninnah became increasingly smug over the fact that she had been given children and Hannah had not. And she used her children as a weapon to grieve Hannah. *"This went on year after year. Whenever Hannah went up to the house of the Lord, her rival provoked her till she wept and would not eat"* (1 Samuel 1:7).

Moved to Desperation

God desired to do something great for Hannah, but first He would need to prepare her for it. God used Peninnah's deplorable behavior to provoke Hannah and irritate her. That is right, it is true that God needed to irritate Hannah. He needed to bring Hannah to the point of desperation, so much so that she would be willing to give Samuel to Him (see 1 Samuel 1:11).

Hannah's pain and disgrace must have been great or she never would have prayed such a prayer. Her desire for a child must have been agonizing, and now she had promised to give that child away? She had no guarantee of ever having more than one child at this point, but her mind was made up. The child would be given to the Lord.

To be without children during that time in history was a great humiliation for a woman. Women of this region were considered children, until they had children. Only as a mother would she be given the respect and authority due an adult. As Hannah got older her disgrace became greater, and she could not escape Peninnah's irritating remarks. This went on for years, until Hannah was so desperate to remove her disgrace that she made a promise to God: if He gave her a son, she would give the boy back to Him.

"In bitterness of soul, Hannah wept much and prayed to the Lord. And she made a vow, saying, 'O Lord Almighty, if you will only look upon your servant's misery and remember me, and not forget your servant, but give her a son, then I will give him to the Lord for all the days of his life, and no razor will ever be used on his head' " (1 Samuel 1:10–11).

A Promise is Born

Hannah, at the very lowest point of her life, prayed her most desperate prayer. She pleaded with God to take away her barrenness and bless her with a son. "Don't forget me!" she cried. She saw everyone around her receiving blessings from God and getting the desires of their hearts, yet she remained barren. She reached the greatest point of misery she had ever known, and laid out her heart before God. Hannah vowed to make the greatest sacrifice any woman could be asked to make. Her sorrow was so great it turned her soul bitter. *Out of this bitter sorrow, a promise was born.*

Hannah's heart was open before God and her tears were never more sincere. Into this precious scene blundered Eli, but he did not see Hannah for what she truly was. She was a woman after God, but Eli mistook the most sincere and heartwrenching moment of her life for that of drunkenness.

"Hannah was praying in her heart, and her lips were moving, but her voice was not heard. Eli thought she was

drunk and said to her, 'How long will you keep on getting drunk? Get rid of your wine' " (1 Samuel 11:13–14).

Perhaps, at times, you have had similar experiences to Hannah's. Your heart was outstretched and open before God, but people around you didn't recognize it as anything out of the ordinary or special. To some you may even seem sinful, but they have judged you incorrectly. The very people we think should recognize our potential are the ones that accuse us of being unspiritual or lacking what it takes to fulfill our potential. Not only did Eli miss the importance of what Hannah was going through, but he also completely misinterpreted her actions toward God.

The Avenue of Offense

At this moment Hannah could have walked away offended, but her need was much too great. She was desperate and wanted what only God could give her, no matter what she had to endure to get it. Some of our greatest blessings come to us through the avenue of offense. Hannah could have walked away, humiliated and discouraged, but she did not. She explained herself to Eli. When he realized how greatly he had misjudged her, he felt so badly that he blessed her instead.

"Go in peace, and may the God of Israel grant you what you have asked of him" (1 Samuel 1:17).

She received a blessing from Eli that she may not have had he not offended her. She received his blessing as being from God and, *"she went her way and ate something, and her face was no longer downcast" (v 18).* She was confident that God had blessed her through Eli even though he had misjudged her. She may never have received what she needed from God, except that her longsuffering brought her the answer to her heart's cry. Hannah was not only a godly woman, but her son would eventually take Eli's place in the temple and restore to Israel everything that Eli's sons had lost.

A Growing Promise

Hannah had already conceived Samuel in her heart before she ever conceived him physically. The dream of him had already been growing inside her. *She was pregnant in the Spirit with the promise of God.* No one, not even Eli, could see the transformation taking place in her heart. It was between her and God alone. She had a secret, a hope, and a dream. When she was referred to as *"barren"* by others seeking to injure her, she clung to the hope of God's enduring faithfulness.

Similarly, when a woman is first pregnant, no one knows she is pregnant except her. No one else can see what is happening inside her. It is her secret. We, too, carry the promises of God secretly inside us. Others can't see anything special in us because God has hidden it from them. They may even misinterpret our desire for God to be something that is sinful or worldly. *No matter how spiritual people are, they cannot see what God has hidden from them.*

Just like a baby hidden in the womb, so are the promises God has given to us. He speaks to us of our future as if to impregnate us with His will and purpose for our lives.

We want to tell the whole world what God has spoken to us. But the promises that the Lord has given to us should be treasured in our hearts and not shared with others who may not be able to see that which God has hidden from them.

Destiny's Irritation

God desires to do great things for us as well. But, like with Hannah, He must drive us to desperation so great that we are willing to give to Him the very thing we are asking Him for.

God uses people like Peninnah, to irritate us (see 1 Samuel 1:6) and provoke us until we are willing to do whatever it takes to receive our destiny in Him. The closer we are to the fulfillment of our destiny, the greater the irritation becomes, until we give up our claims to our destiny. We give up our dreams in exchange for His will; our ambitions for His plan.

In return, we not only receive what we were hoping for, but more than we have even dreamt of. Hannah not only got the son she desired, but her family line was established, through Samuel, as priests to the Lord forever. In addition to Samuel, she was also blessed with five other children.

God desires to do much more through us than we think is possible, but it must be done His way. Through His mercy, He keeps us from accepting less than all He has for us. All Hannah wanted was a son, but God wanted a prophet for His people and a friend for Himself.

Promise Through the Pain

"In bitterness of soul Hannah wept much and prayed to the Lord" (1 Samuel 1:10).

I have heard people say that God would not do anything to them that would cause them to suffer. They say, "God wants to bless me!" and I say, yes, God does want to bless us, but some of our greatest blessings come out of our greatest pain. If we do not experience the pain, it is more difficult for us to appreciate the blessings we are given. It did not please God to cause Hannah such misery, but He could see the future and He needed Samuel. The only way He could get the promise to her was through the pain.

God *does* see your struggle and your pain; He hurts with you and weeps with you. He is begging you not to give up, because He can see your future and it is great! *"For I know the plans I have for you," declares the Lord, "plans to prosper you and not to harm you, plans to give you a future and a hope" (Jeremiah 29:11).*

The Lord's presence remained with all of Israel through Samuel, because Hannah chose not to give up on the dream she had in her heart. She chose to believe that God loved her and saw her as special even when others did not.

If the Lord has given you a dream or a promise of something so wonderful that others cannot receive it, keep it hidden in your heart as a secret treasure, until the moment of its birth. Some things should be kept between you and the Lord. He is jealous for your heart and wants you to Himself. Do not look for acceptance from anyone but Him; hold onto the God who loves you. His will *will* be done!

Pray this with me:

Dear Father,

Keep alive in me all that You have promised me. Cause all the circumstances that I must walk through to turn me toward You, not away from You. Help me to seek You and Your approval, and not the approval of others.

Open the Door to Your Destiny

Chapter Five

KEEP YOUR LAMPS BURNING

God is asking you to make yourself ready for service to the King and, with a watchful attitude, to wait on Him. He wants you to keep your lamp burning . . . be dressed and ready for service (see Luke 12:35) and wait for Him to call you to serve Him.

Be Dressed and Ready for Service

O ur Father is asking us to prepare ourselves and be ready for Him to open the door to our destiny. There is a kingdom principle of preparation before service. It is during this time when God's will becomes our own. Our own ideas and plans for our lives are surrendered and we take on God's plan for us—much like you would take off one outfit and put on another.

The Lord demands that we take off all *self-righteousness* and put on His garment of righteousness through grace alone. We must believe in and rely on Christ's sacrifice on the cross to save us and fulfill us. That is *too* simple, isn't it? Many think it is too simple and they end up relying on their own works to make themselves ready for the service of the King. They feel they have so much to offer Him that, of course, He would call on them to serve. It is not until we discard our own worthiness, and realize that we are nothing without Him, that He calls us into His service.

In Luke 9:23 the Lord says, *"If anyone would come after me, he must deny himself."* We must deny ourselves to follow Him. We must deny our own righteousness, our own plans and ideas about ourselves and our future. We think that our gifts and our talents are so valuable to God that He needs us. It is not our gifts and talents that make us valuable to Him, but it is us. He wants and needs *us*, not what we have to offer Him. Moreover, our Lord often uses us for something we have no natural talent for. If you can sing, get ready to preach, or vice versa, because God wants the glory for what He does. So He strips us of everything we deem worthy, and He replaces it with His own plans and ideas of how He will use us.

We may think that, because we have an incredible singing voice, God would choose to use us in music. God loves a challenge and He will close one door just to open the door to something you have never done before. He will open the door for you to do something that you may be afraid to do. He loves to throw us into situations that will necessitate our reliance on

Him in order to accomplish the task He has given us to do. In this way He keeps us linked to Him.

"This is Something We Can Use!"

God gave me a dream once that impacted my life greatly and gave me peace in the midst of struggling with my life's purpose. In the dream I walked into a college classroom where a professor was down front lecturing to his class. After class, I brought to him a large painting that I had painted which I thought was very beautiful. I showed it to him, but he decided that it was not of any value. As he continued to study my painting, he noticed on one corner that there was another painting underneath the one I had painted. He began ripping off the picture I had painted and, with astonishment, he discovered a highly valuable picture underneath it. As I was struggling to get over the shock of having him rip up my picture, he proclaimed, *"Now, this is something we can use!"*

When I woke from the dream, I began to pray. The Lord told me that the dream represented the work He would do in my life to prepare me for my destiny. He said that what I considered to be my greatest contribution to the body of Christ would not be, but He had placed a gift deep down inside of me that would be even more valuable to His people.

I knew then that all that I had been striving to accomplish using my most obvious gifts and talents would not be what He would call into service. I would have to be stripped of all that I had accomplished and be reclothed in His garments and further fashioned into His image.

Disrobing

In the first few moments after arriving at the hospital to give birth, you are asked to disrobe. They want you in the clothes that they have provided for you. No matter how fancy or expensive *our* clothes might be, they are not suitable for giving birth.

"Then he said to his servants, 'The wedding banquet is ready, but those I invited did not deserve to come. Go to the street corners and invite to the banquet anyone you find.' So the servants went out into the streets and gathered all the people they could find, both good and bad, and the wedding hall was filled with guests.

"But when the king came in to see the guests, he noticed a man there who was not wearing wedding clothes. 'Friend,' he asked, 'how did you get in here without wedding clothes?' The man was speechless" (Matthew 22:8–12).

In this parable Jesus talks about the people who were the original guests at the banquet but refused to come to the feast He had prepared for them. They simply refused to come (see Matthew 22:2–7). The Bridegroom decided to open the feast to anyone who would come. The wedding hall was filled, but he noticed that one man who came to the wedding was not dressed in wedding clothes.

We are not told why the man chose not to put on wedding clothes, but we are told what happened to him because he did not (see Matthew 22:13). He was asked in Matthew 22:12

why, but he was speechless; he had no answer. Seemingly, all he had to do was put on the garment. But first he would have to take off *his* clothes. He would need to disrobe. His clothes represented what he had done for himself, his own righteousness. He could not put on the robe provided for him unless he first gave up his own wardrobe. This was something that he was unwilling to do.

His clothes were probably dirty and tattered and practically rags, but he clung to them. He pulled together the torn pieces of his garment so that others would not see his nakedness. His clothing looked frightful to the host, but represented a great deal to the man wearing them. This is much like the self-justification of our own lives, which becomes our ticket to heaven, instead of Christ's sacrifice on the cross. We need to clothe ourselves in Christ alone. We must say goodbye to pride that seeks to justify our sin instead of surrendering it at the foot of the cross, and then receive Christ's sacrifice alone as atonement for our sins.

We need to let go of our works and rely only on the robe He provided for us as a gift. That robe was and is the only thing that will make us acceptable to our host at the wedding supper of the Lamb. Any other robe of our own making is as filthy rags to Him, even though it appears appealing to us and to others.

Jesus is the robe of righteousness that is provided for us. That is why the Jews refused to come, because they refused to accept Jesus. So God (our host) turned to us, the Gentiles. But whether we are Jew or Gentile, male or female, rich or poor, it does not matter. What matters is that we are clothed in Christ (see Galatians 3:28–29).

This man said he would come to the banquet, but he wanted to get there his own way. He could not let go of his own works or his self-righteousness. He was probably unconscious of the fact that he was improperly dressed. He, through his eyes of pride, might have thought his outfit to be above the rest.

That is what Jesus was trying to show the Pharisees by using this parable. He desperately wanted them to see that they were only wearing rags. But they could not let go of their rags because of their pride. Pride tries to act as our friend, but it is really our greatest enemy. Our sin is hidden by our pride. Pride makes excuses for our sin. *"For in his own eyes he flatters himself too much to detect or hate his sin" (Psalm 36:2).*

Our pride is what keeps us from going down to the altar when a call is made. It keeps us from receiving from God, because we fear what others will think of us. Our pride keeps us from receiving more of Jesus, and it will also keep us from receiving the promises of God. We, as Christians, are all wearing the same robe. None of us are righteous except through His sacrifice (see Romans 3:23–24), so why do we keep on trying to be better than one another?

Grace is the great equalizer that allows us to distinguish others as more important than ourselves (see Philippians 2:3), which is the essence of the kingdom of God. We, as the people of God, need to see the pride within ourselves as the greatest enemy we fight, and *we need to be aggressive in loving those whom the spirit of pride causes us to feel superior to.* This isn't just a charitable love, but brotherly love—a love that makes them feel good about themselves. This is not the kind of love that makes us feel better about ourselves because we were willing to love someone we consider to be lower than ourselves. When we put on Christ's sacrifice, we put on His love, His grace, and His mercy for our fellow man. And who is our fellow man? Anyone born of a woman!

He Will Lift Us Up

We know that we cannot give birth in the natural without first disrobing. In the same way, we cannot possibly give birth to anything of God without disrobing in the spirit. When we disrobe in the spirit, we give up everything that we have done for ourselves and everything we have done for God. We hold nothing to ourselves to make us righteous, other than the sacrifice of Christ's death. It is *His* righteousness, and His only, that will produce anything lasting in our lives. When we wash our hands of the sin of pride, and mourn over the condition of our hearts, then He will lift us up. And then we will see the fulfillment of God's promises; then we will give birth!

"I am the vine; you are branches. If a man remains in me and I in him, he will bear much fruit; apart from me you can do nothing. If anyone does not remain in me, he is like a branch that is thrown away and withers; such branches are picked up, thrown into the fire and are burned" (John 15:5–6).

We are told in Matthew 22:13, that the improperly dressed man was tied hand and foot, then thrown outside, where there was weeping and gnashing of teeth. He was separated from God to show him his need of God. The pain of the experience brought weeping and fear (gnashing of teeth). In John 15:6 we read that the branches that are not connected to Christ will be burned. I believe that God puts us through a refining process in the fire, and all that does not belong to Him will be burned. When this burning process is finished, we are prepared for all that He has for us. What is left of us is Him. In humility, we are obedient servants to our master . . . we are ready to wear the robe of His choice, not our own. We are submitted to Him, and He will lift us up.

Pray this with me:

Dearest Father,

Please forgive me for trying to do things on my own. Forgive me for the sin of pride. Show me anything in my heart that is not pleasing to You. Do what You have to do in me to fulfill the promise You have made to me.

~ Chapter Six ~

GOD WANTS FIRST PLACE

To fulfill our destiny, we may be asked to put aside the things we are known for in order to experience the enjoyment of working alongside our heavenly Father.

The Lord asked me several times to write a book. Even though I said "yes" to Him, I continued to procrastinate. I intended to write it, but there just was not time. For years I put it off, until one day a lady prophesied to me, "Write the book!" It was such a powerful word that it shook me. I had no doubt that God was speaking to me through her. It was not a "God bless you" kind of word, but more of a rebuke. After she spoke to me, I actually had a fear of *not* writing it, but it was a good kind of fear. It was the same type of fear you get when your earthly parent scolds you. So I began to write.

At first, I stumbled around, not having a clue of the direction the Lord wanted me to take. I was not enjoying writing, either; it felt like a chore. I sought the Lord for an answer. I thought, "If God told me to write, why isn't He helping me?" *I needed to dive into God and completely immerse myself in Him and His Word.* I needed to change my life to make it completely focused on this task.

My time became the first thing that He took control of. He spoke to me and said, *"You can be a Mary or a Martha, but you can never be both!"* To me that meant, my time could be spent sewing, crafting or decorating (all the things I enjoyed) or I could give up all those earthly pleasures to spend time in His presence studying the Word and writing. My social life was another thing He conquered. I had to curb my time spent with my friends, which caused me to become well acquainted with loneliness.

Another sacrifice needed to be made—my time spent working outside the home. This was especially hard because I enjoyed working and our family needed the extra income. It took faith to make these changes, but my life belonged to God and I let Him control it.

Time and again I would get caught up in wanting to busy myself with prayer groups, good causes and school activities. Since my time belonged to God, I tried to live by these words: *"In his heart a man plans his course, but the Lord determines his steps" (Proverbs 16:9).* And so, again and again, He would say "no" to my business and "yes" to time spent with Him.

The Good or the Great

How easy it is to get so caught up in doing the good that you neglect the great. In Luke, chapter ten, Jesus and His disciples were traveling when they came to the village where two sisters, Mary and Martha, lived. Martha opened their home up to the travelers. She wished to make their stay at her home very nice; she wanted very much to please the Lord.

"She had a sister called Mary, who sat at the Lord's feet listening to what he said. But Martha was distracted by all the preparations that had to be made" (Luke 10:39–40).

Martha was upset that Mary would not help her. When she approached Jesus about her distress, He said, *"Only one thing is needed. Mary has chosen what is better, and it will not be taken from her" (Luke 10:42).*

Mary chose what was better—to sit in the Lord's presence. Even if the work went undone, the Lord did not care. It was more important to Him that they spent their time *with* Him and not just *serving* Him. Jesus desired to have Martha sit with Him, too. Mary was no more special to Jesus than Martha was. He wanted to spend time with both of them. He is calling all of us to stop *doing things* for Him and start *spending time* with Him. We will never be able to fulfill our callings if we do not give Him first place.

Martha was so distracted by the preparations she was making for Jesus that she missed out on her destiny. She missed the point of Jesus' visit to their home. He did not want a maid, but a friend!

Years ago the Lord came to me in a very powerful way. He rolled over my body with wave after wave of His presence. It was the first time that I had ever experienced His power in that way. I was awed by His power and I (like Peter) thought that God wanted me to do something for Him. I asked Him expectantly, "Lord, what do you want me to do for You?" His answer set my heart spinning. He said, "Just experience me." I, like Martha, missed the point of His visit. He just wanted me to experience His presence and get acquainted with Him. Since that time I have gotten accustomed to experiencing His presence, so much so that I simply cannot live without it. *Nothing we do for Him could replace the time spent with Him. We are more important to Him than anything He needs done.*

He is the Prize

To fulfill our destiny in Him, we may be asked to put aside those things we are known for. What are we known for? The things we do! People admire doers. We give awards to do-gooders. *The only reward we get for spending time with God is spending time with God. But, oh, what a reward! He is the prize! He is the pearl of great price!*

"Again, the kingdom of heaven is like a merchant looking for fine pearls. When he found one of great value, he went away and sold everything he had and bought it" (Matthew 13:45–46).

When we discover the joy of friendship with God, we have a choice to make. Do we give up all the things we enjoy and grasp with all our might this pearl of great price, or do we get distracted by life and miss out on Him? Was it wrong for Martha to want to "prepare" things for Jesus and make things nice for Him? No, but it was not what He wanted from her. He did not come to their house for a dinner, but for the fellowship of His friends.

Overflowing Love

I realized that I would never fulfill my destiny *in God* unless I first *obeyed God*. I had a hunger inside of me to follow the call He placed on my heart; what was that call? It was to become one with Him in thought, word and deed. Everything else I would ever do for Him would flow out of that relationship. It had to come out of the overflow of a full heart. *Like a river overflowing its banks, we must minister for Him out of our fullness of Him.*

You can not serve tea from an empty teapot! Even our ministry to our family and friends must come from our overflowing fullness of God's presence in our lives. He is all we have to offer the world, so we must be full of Him in order to give Him to others.

"Obedience is better than sacrifice" (1 Samuel 15:22). If He says "love me," then we must love Him, even if it means we sacrifice our sacrifices. Our sacrifices are the "preparations" that we have made on our own. I realize that sometimes things have to get done, God knows this. I am sure that after His visit with Mary and Martha, He would release them to fix

the dinner. Our sacrifice must come from our obedience to Him and our relationship with Him. When we give Him first place over our other activities, then He empowers us to do those activities and more.

The Spirit or the Flesh?

When we sow to the flesh we reap from the flesh, but when we sow to the Spirit we reap from the Spirit (see Galatians 6:8). When we spend time with God, our flesh decreases and our spirit increases. When our spirit increases, we know and hear God better. Even though God had forcefully requested that I write this book, He would not allow me to do it without Him. His request drove me deeper into Him and drove out all of the things that were distracting me from Him.

God does not just desire people who will work for Him, but He desires that our work for Him should draw us to Him. When we rely on the arm of the flesh to fulfill our calling, we offend God. He will confound our efforts until we stop and seek Him.

We cannot produce in the flesh what can only be birthed in the Spirit. *"Are you so foolish? After beginning in the Spirit, are you now trying to attain your goal by human effort?" (Galatians 3:3).* Writing became my joy, not my job. Whatever the Lord has asked you to do, He did not intend for you to do it without Him.

Our service for Him must be birthed out of our passion for Him. *"If you love me, you will obey me" (John 14:15).* You will not be able to stop yourself from obeying Him, because you will be so full of Him. When you see a need, you will run to meet it. You will be doing it with more love than you ever thought you were capable of. Indeed, it will be His love working through you, not your own. And *His* love is without measure!

Pray this with me:

Dear Father,

I repent now of trying to fulfill Your work through my own strength. Teach me the ways of Your Spirit and help me to follow Your lead. I want to be one with You in thought, word and deed.

~ Chapter Seven ~

HUMILITY
PRECEDES HONOR

Whatever honor we receive, we must present as a gift to the One we honor.

"When someone invites you to a wedding feast, do not take the place of honor" (Luke 14:8).

The desire to be honored seems to have been in us since birth. Even the most reserved people do desire a little recognition now and then. This desire is not abnormal or wrong, but is a part of our own natural human desire to be loved. However, the desire for recognition or honor can be dangerous for us if we manipulate people in order to receive it. Moreover, if we do have the natural desire to be honored, we should never strive for it. We will enjoy it much more if it comes in God's timing and for His purpose, and if it is a gift we are given and not something we have demanded of people.

God desires to honor His children, but we must never strive for honor. Striving leads to an ambitious mindset which is never satisfied. God desires to raise up people who have chosen the lowly places in life, to give them honor. *"But when you are invited take the lowest place, so that when your host comes, he will say to you, 'Friend, move up to a better place.' Then you will be honored in the presence of all your fellow guests"* (Luke 14:10).

The Purpose for Honor

God does not intend to raise us up just so we can be recognized. He gives us a platform, that we may raise others up, as well. He frees you to help Him free others. Whatever influence you have, use it to benefit others. *"Each of you should look not only to your own interests, but also to the interests of others"* (Philippians 2:4). In so doing, whatever glory you might receive, you give back to your heavenly Father; you will see the purpose of influence and honor. It is not about you or I, but all glory and honor belongs to Him. Therefore, any glory or honor we might receive, we need to give back to Him, because without Him it would not have been possible. All things are summed up in Him (see Revelation 4:10).

If we are standing in the light of His majesty and glory, we could never accept any honor for ourselves. *Everything we have accomplished on this earth will be as nothing in view of His throne.*

"You are worthy, our Lord and God, to receive glory and honor and power, for you created all things, and by your will they were created and have their being" (Revelation 4:11).

By Him were all things created; to Him does all glory belong! As long as we are giving all glory back to God, we are safe from the eroding influences of pride. And He will give us the platform we need to accomplish His purposes. Any influence or authority we are given in this life is a gift from the Father—a gift, as much as a responsibility, to accomplish His purposes.

As long as we keep His kingdom purposes in mind, and not our own fleshly desires, the adulation we receive from people will not corrupt us. We will see that the favor we have been given with people is given for the purpose of building up His kingdom and His people.

People do not have to attend our churches, listen to our sermons or read our books. They do so because, through our meager efforts, God has chosen to build up others. He chooses to use us to bless His people. If God has blessed you with a ministry, then keep in mind that it is to minister to His people, not to make you great! Ministry is a great responsibility . . . but also a great blessing. It is a blessing to minister to God's dear people and have Him bless that ministry. It is a thrill like no other to do the will of the Father and for Him to say, *well done, good and faithful servant.*

Do Not Fear

There are millions of people on this earth who need to know God. They are desperate to know that God loves them. God wants us to tell them that He knows them and He loves them. If we keep in mind that all we do is done for His people and for His glory, we will not fear. We will know that it is not about us, but about His love for His people. We are just ambassadors of that love—the messengers who bring His message.

We are God's tool, much like a pen writes on paper. We do not glorify or thank the pen for the words on a page. The pen did not originate the writing. It was merely the tool the author used to write a message. We are simply a tool! The tool has no reason to fear anything, because whether the message we bring is accepted or rejected, it is not up to us, but God. If people accept it, they will receive the reward God has promised. If it is rejected, they are answerable to God. They are not rejecting you, but the message you bring. You cannot force them to receive, it is only by God's grace that they can receive—not by anything we do or say. Do not take it personally and do not fear.

An Act of Worship

"And there before me was a throne in heaven with someone sitting on it. Surrounding the throne were twenty-four other thrones, and seated on them were twenty-four elders. They were dressed in white and had crowns of gold on their heads" (Revelation 4:2–4).

"Whenever the living creatures give glory, honor and thanks to him who sits on the throne and who lives forever and ever, the twenty-four elders fall down before him who sits on the throne, and worship him who lives forever and ever. They lay their crowns before the throne and say; 'You are worthy, our Lord and God, to receive glory and honor and power, for you created all things, and by your will they were created and have their being' " (Revelation 4:9–11).

As an act of love and reverence, the elders took off their crowns, laid them before the throne, and fell down before Him who sits on the throne. They did not do this just once, but it was done every time the living creatures gave Him glory. When God was being praised, they could not stay seated; they could not resist the desire to worship and honor God.

They took off their crowns, which represented their honor, and laid them at His feet. To me this symbolizes the surrender of their own personal honor to the God they loved, and He meant more to them than their own personal honor. Whatever honor they had received, they presented as a gift to the God they honored.

All of the elders had been given thrones, which symbolized their positions. But not even their positions kept them from worshiping God. They could not stay on their thrones while He was being worshiped. Their thrones meant nothing to them in the light of His glory and majesty.

Likewise, the elders' positions or the honor they were given served not to puff them up, but became only tools for them to worship their God. Any position they had been given or honor they had acquired was used simply to worship God.

We too must never serve our positions, but rather use them as a platform to love our God. The honor He has given each one of us must be surrendered back to Him continually, to show Him He is forever first in our hearts. Our position of honor must mean very little to us compared to our love and adoration for our Lord.

It's Not About Us

It is not about us, but it is about Him and His people—His kingdom! Everything we do must be done out of an obedient heart for the building up of His kingdom and for His glory. When this is your heart's cry, you need not fear fire or flood, misunderstandings or rejection. Your God is in control of your life and He will never let you fall beyond His reach or ability to restore you into His presence again.

Pray this with me:

Dear Father,

Let everything I do glorify You! Help me to submit all of my heart to You. Let my life be the crown that I lay down at Your throne, and may my life please You.

Preparing for Your Destiny

~ Chapter Eight ~

THE THREE BATTLES OF GREATNESS

God recognized Jesus publicly as being His own Son, a Son He loved and was proud of. This blessing was tested by Satan when He endured the testing (see Luke 4:1–13).

"When all the people were being baptized, Jesus was baptized too. And as he was praying heaven was opened and the Holy Spirit descended on him in bodily form like a dove. And a voice came from heaven: 'You are my Son, whom I love; with you I am well pleased' " (Luke 3:21–22).

*J*esus got in line with the rest of the people being baptized. He was the Son of God, yet He blended in as one of the crowd. He knew His destiny, He knew who He was, but He sought to be treated like everyone else until the time of His ministry was to begin. Suddenly, He is plucked out of the crowd and introduced as God's own Son.

This was not a revelation for Jesus' benefit; He had always known whose Son He was. But this was His introduction to the world. God spoke to all present, "This is my beloved Son, I love Him and I am pleased with Him." It was His time of recognition; the time His Father was waiting for. God had been wishing to publicly acclaim Him, to show His Son how much He loved Him. Now, He finally could.

Test Number One: Prove It!

"The devil said to him, 'If you are the Son of God, tell this stone to become bread' " (Luke 4:3).

God declared to all that Jesus was His Son, and that is exactly who He was. But in Luke 4:3, Satan wanted Jesus to prove it. How often we seem to struggle with the same testing. God declares marvelous words over us, but then those words are tested. One moment we are standing in the awe of God's love for us, and then in the next moment utter chaos breaks loose against us. This pattern is all too familiar to me in my life: I get a word, then comes the test. I have come to expect it. And when the time of testing has passed, I know more clearly who I am and why I have been placed in the position I am in.

Satan wanted Christ to prove who He was. How often we are faced with the temptation of proving that we are anointed, and that God is with us. God will often allow people to view us as insignificant to test our humility. We will please our Father by ignoring Satan's pull to try and prove our significancy to them. Christ refused to fall into this snare of Satan by saying, "No, thank you, I'm not *that* hungry." He refused Satan's attempt to get Him to prove Himself; we must refuse, also.

It is not our job to prove ourselves; when we try to, it displeases God. He is more pleased when we think of ourselves as ordinary. You could be the next great apostle or teacher to appear on the world scene, but you would please God more if you remain hidden and humble until He is ready to establish your ministry publicly.

Test Number Two: Premature Promises

"The devil led him up to a high place and showed him in an instant all the kingdoms of the world. And he said to him, 'I will give you all their authority and splendor, for it has been given to me, and I can give it to anyone I want to. So if you worship me, it will all be yours'" (Luke 4:5–7).

The second test for Jesus was that of having the promises of God granted prematurely. Satan wanted to give Jesus all that was His to inherit eventually anyway. Satan did not want Christ to inherit anything, he just wanted control over His destiny. There was a price Christ paid for the kingdom He would inherit. That price was His life, and we were His reward.

God has a plan and a destiny for each of us, but we must be patient and arrive at our destiny by the means the Lord has designed for us. There is a price to be paid for the anointing that God gives; we must pay whatever price we are asked to pay. Satan knows your destiny probably better than you do, and if he can get you to jump the gun, then he, not God, has control of your destiny.

God gave us a promise for our perseverance in James 1:4, when He said, "Perseverance must finish its work so that you may be mature and complete, not lacking anything." It is not our gifts that God seeks to develop in us as much as it is our character.

Test Number Three: The Presumptuous Attitude

"If you are the Son of God," he said, "throw yourself down from here. For it is written, 'He will command his angels concerning you to guard you carefully'" (Luke 4:9–10).

Test number three was even more diabolical and subtle—he used the Word of God. Again he strikes at the words God spoke over Him, *"If you are the Son of God,"* and this time it was to threaten His life.

Satan aspired to push Jesus into testing the Word that God had spoken over Him. But it never works to move out into your calling before your character has been proven. It is like trying to sail a ship without a rudder. You may sail the boat, but you won't get anywhere. Usually this battle is fought when our wait has been the longest and our patience is quite strained. When we are at our weakest, the enemy comes in like a flood.

Our toughest battles are fought when we are at our weakest because, *"When I am weak, then I am strong" (2 Corinthians 12:10)*. Even when we are starving and weak, God will allow us to be tested. But, was Christ *really* weak at this time? His body may have been weakened, but I believe His Spirit was strong and fighting His battles for Him. He was able to use simple words of Scripture to destroy the deceptions of Satan, because God was with Him.

Moreover, we can fight the enemy when we are weak, with even the simplest of weapons. When Satan says we will never see the promises of God fulfilled if we wait on Him, we can say simply, "That's a lie!" God's words are true! I will see the salvation of the Lord!

Just Keep Breathing

Picture Christ on top of the highest point of the temple. He is exhausted to the point of fainting; He just wants this testing to be over with. Satan is using the same Scripture that was prophesied to Him; he says in essence, *Okay, I will agree that You are the Son of God, but here is what they say the Christ will be able to do, so go ahead and try it. Why not just test God to see if what He says about You is true?*

Even with the degree of oppression Christ must have been under, He decided He'd had enough. All He wanted was for Satan to leave Him alone. Does that sound familiar? "I just want this all to be over!" Have you felt like that—exhausted and wanting the testing to end, to be over? When there is nothing left of us but air, then we just breathe. Christ spoke one more Scripture that would refute His tempter. He said, "I cannot test God, because the Bible says not to." Then the devil left him (see Luke 4:13).

Friend, the testing you endure is not for God's benefit, but for yours. It is in the midst of the battle that you find out who you really are. You find out what great strength lies within you. It is then that you see that you can do all things through Christ who strengthens you (see Philippians 4:13). When you are finished with your time of testing, you will then have experience at fighting the enemy that will carry you through to the fulfillment of your destiny.

Pray this with me:

Dear Father,

Please help me to finish the course You have set before me. May I not get ahead of You or leave You behind. Forgive my anxious thoughts, and help me trust You and stand strong in the time of testing.

Chapter Nine

PERFECTED LOVE

Offense does not come to ruin your life, but to enhance it. However, our reaction to that offense will determine how long it will take us to fulfill our destiny. It is necessary for us to become, as my pastor puts it, "unoffendable."

*T*he areas in our lives where we are easily offended are areas where we are vulnerable to attack, and the Lord desires to strengthen us in those areas. If we are a little too sensitive about a particular issue, it is usually because it is an area of our life that we need to change. When we become unaffected by the enemy's tactics against us, or unmoved by his hurtful darts, it is then that we realize that God has made us strong in that area.

God seeks to perfect His love in our hearts. He cannot do that without bringing some offensive people into our lives—people who know how to trip those peculiar little buttons in our hearts that send us reeling into self-pity and offense. We can run away from these people, but we will just run into the same type of person later on. The best thing to do when we are offended is to run into our Savior's arms. It is there He can bring His wisdom into our lives and change our hearts. Do not look at what was wrong with the other person, because God is seeking to perfect the work He is doing in you (see Romans 8:29). Trust Him and you will indeed become unoffendable.

Focusing on Our Destiny

Our goal should be to measure up to God's plan for us—not to remain the same, but to become stronger in Him. We cannot do that without enduring the trials that God brings into our lives to change us. Offense is the thermometer that lets us know how we have changed. Offense lets us know areas of our hearts where we are vulnerable to cold love, where we need the heating pad of God's grace to warm our hearts to make us vessels of His love to the world!

If we keep the purposes of God in the forefront of our minds, it makes it easier to endure the testing that offense brings into our lives. Our focus must be on God and on His plan for our lives, not on the conditions around us. God has a specific plan for you and He will do whatever it takes to fulfill that plan in order to complete the process of forming you into *"the likeness of his Son" (Romans 8:29).*

God may appear to be harder on you than He is on other people around you. However, you may accomplish more in your future than they will in theirs. And the endeavors you undertake will require a deeper level of character. Do not compare or measure yourself by the people around you. God has a specific purpose for you. That purpose will *always* begin and end in Him.

God is the only one who can open doors for you (see Romans 8:30). Do not look to man to do it and do not blame them when they don't. *God is the only one who will make a way for your destiny.* He will not allow you to get there without Him, but will wait until you are ready to properly *care* for the desires of your heart (see 2 Timothy 3:17).

Often God will shut the door that you desire Him to open, only to open an even better one at a later time. Trust Him, and do not become discouraged when things don't turn out as you wished they would have. *"And we know that in all things God works for the good of those who love him, who have been called according to his purpose" (Romans 8:28).* His way is always right.

Beware of Hidden Offense

When the Lord sent messengers to a Samaritan village in Luke 9:51–56, they found that the Lord was unwelcome there. The disciples wanted to call down fire from heaven to destroy the village, but the Lord rebuked them.

This incident became a test for His disciples. Why were the disciples so ready to destroy this village? They had been rejected by other cities and had not wished to see them destroyed. However, this was a Samaritan village and the Jews did not like the Samaritans. They had offense in their hearts toward them! They were willing to minister to the

Samaritans out of an attitude of pity for them, but when their good intentions were rejected, they took offense.

We need to watch out for hidden offense and wrong attitudes that will cause us to react in a way that would bring the Lord's rebuke on us. These are the areas of our hearts the Lord seeks to change. He is working to perfect our love to the extent that people will find themselves copying us in behavior, as we model the love of Christ. Our role model for our love walk *is Christ*. Friends, God wants to mold you into the image of His unoffendable Son. Let Him do it!

Please pray this with me:

Dear Father,
Help me to be like Your Son Jesus. Give me an unoffendable heart so that I can be used to show the world Your heart.

Chapter Ten

THANK YOUR OFFENDERS

God loves to use our enemies to bless us. Moreover, He loves to show us off right in front of their eyes. God will send us like sheep among wolves in order to show His favor toward us. He sends us into the darkness to make His light in us shine brighter.

"You prepare a table before me in the presence of my enemies" (Psalm 23:5).

We are sent into the desert and instructed to spring forth as a mighty river of living water. In the brightness of day, a lamp is not as useful, but during the darkness of night we cannot see without it. It is through the tough times that we see God's power manifest in the greatest degree.

In Acts, chapter five, Peter and the other apostles were arrested by the Sadducees and the high priest, who had the disciples thrown into prison. *"But during the night an angel of the Lord opened the doors of the jail and brought them out"(Acts 5:19).* They were then instructed to, *"Go, stand in the temple courts and tell the people the full message of this new life"(Acts 5:20).*

Immediately, on being miraculously led out of jail, they were told to go back to the temple—the very place where the Sadducees were. God did not set them free to hide out in the wilderness, but to go back to the place where they were the most vulnerable to attack. They were told to go to the place where they might have the greatest fear, and then preach fully the gospel of Jesus Christ.

God loves to display His power by taking us into the lion's den and then keeping us safe with His hand. *"So do not fear, for I am with you; do not be dismayed, for I am your God. I will strengthen you and help you; I will uphold you with my righteous right hand" (Isaiah 41:10).*

Personal History

My life has been greatly impacted by the history of my great-great-great grandparents, John and Cynthia Hoskin, who came to America from Sweden in 1872 with a passion in their hearts to bring the gospel to the early settlers here. They desired to go as far west as they could, that they might reach the people they felt had the greatest need.

On the way out west, they got as far as northern Nebraska, where they were held up for months by the worst blizzard in Nebraska's history. They stayed in the homes of the settlers there. Soon they realized that God had intended for them to stay in Nebraska—so they decided to bloom where they were planted and produce fruit right where they were. They started a ministry that evolved into a thriving church. Many pioneers were saved under their ministry, and the anointing of God flowed in their services. If it had not been for the storm, they would have missed the blessings that God had in store for them there.

Out of the greatest storms in our lives come the greatest blessings. The more impossible the situation seems, the more determined God is to see you do what He has said you would do. With an audience of impossibilities, God puts on a display of His power to protect you.

Get Back on Your Horse!

Let us go back to Acts, chapter five. The apostles did not let the difficulties of their situation keep them from doing God's will. When they were thrown off their horses, they got right back on. I mean, God would not let the Sadducees keep them from fulfilling their call. Due to their determination to obey God rather than men (see Acts 5:29), they saw God's divine intervention (see Acts 5:40). They were able to share the message of Jesus Christ with the Sadducees. And they were delivered once again from the Sadducees' hands, this time by a Pharisee named Gamaliel, as they continued to spread the message of the gospel.

Why did God tell them to go to the temple? Why did He not keep them from further possible imprisonment? I believe it was because God wanted to display His power to them. He led them right to the front door of their enemies and then He blessed them. He gave the disciples favor with Gamaliel so their enemies could not touch them. Meanwhile, they had ample opportunity to present the gospel in the presence of their enemies. Again I quote Psalm 23:5, *"You prepare a table before me in the presence of my enemies."*

Let Them Curse

The more people fuss and declare the impossibilities of your situation, the more determined God is to see you through it, and the more He will bless you. Let them try and discourage you; God is keeping score. The more graciously you endure the scourge of your enemies, the more determined God is to bless you.

So, let your enemies rage against you, for they shall surely be put to shame and disgraced (see Isaiah 41:11). God will raise you up with His mighty right hand and declare, *"Do not fear; I will help you" (Isaiah 41:13)*. Do not let your enemies stop you from fulfilling your call! God will use the curses they have thrown at you today as the excuse to bless you tomorrow.

In Second Samuel, chapter sixteen, David left the city of Jerusalem to escape from his son Absalom, who was taking over the city. As David approached the city of Bahurim, a man from the clan of Saul's family, Shimei, came out to meet them. He cursed David as he came out, and pelted him with stones. David's men were appalled and wanted to kill Shimei, but David would not let them. He said, *"Leave him alone; let him curse, for the Lord has told him to. It may be that the*

Lord will see my distress and repay me with good for the cursing I am receiving today" (2 Samuel 16:11–12).

God is keeping score and He will pay you back with heavenly blessings for the scourge you have received from your enemies. This is part of the birth process. The offenses we have received from others simply open our hearts to receive more of the anointing into our lives. We will be eating a feast of His power and presence while our enemies look on, unable to understand why we have been chosen to receive such blessing. Little did they know it was their reproach against us that made us a target for God's blessing. It was their betrayal that brought God's best blessings to our doorstep!

Thank your offenders! The more they curse you, the more God will bless you. It only gives God an excuse to favor you.

Chapter Eleven

THE KEY TO
YOUR DESTINY

*Learning to honor the authority that God has placed
you under could be the key that unlocks the door to your
destiny!*

efore God promotes us, we will be tested in
the area of authority. He will test us to see if
we will respect and obey those in authority over us, even when
we disagree with their decisions. God blessed Saul when He
put Samuel in authority over him, but Saul did not seem to
realize it (see 1 Samuel 15:1). As king, Saul was given
authority over the kingdom of Israel, but he was still under the
authority of Samuel, whose job it was to lead and guide Saul.

It was Samuel's place to bless Saul with God's favor in the
battles he would fight. And it was Samuel who spoke and gave
Saul the word of the Lord. God used Samuel to give direction

and wisdom to Saul's leadership, and to tell him when he should fight and when he should not. Even though Saul was king of Israel, God was in control. God made Saul king but He wanted Saul to work with Samuel to guide the people into all that He had for them.

For Men or For God

In 1 Samuel 13:6–10, we see Saul's first act of disobedience toward the authority that God had established for him. When Saul saw his men leaving him, and Samuel had not yet come to bless them with a burnt offering, he was distressed. He took matters into his own hands and offered the burnt sacrifice himself. Out of fear, because his men were leaving, he stepped out of the realm of the authority that God had established for him.

Just as Saul finished making the offering, Samuel arrived, and Saul went out to greet him. *"'What have you done?' asked Samuel. Saul replied, 'When I saw that the men were scattering, and that you did not come at the set time, and that the Philistines were assembling at Micmash, I thought, "Now the Philistines will come down against me at Gilgal, and I have not sought the Lord's favor. So I felt compelled to offer the burnt offering" ' "* (1 Samuel 13:6–10).

Saul became impatient with the leadership God had put in authority over him. He saw that the needs of the men he led were not being met by Samuel. His eyes were on the situation at hand and not on God's abilities. The needs of his men were not being met, but the authority to meet their needs had not been given to Saul. God had given that place to Samuel, and even if he was late in performing his duties, it was not Saul's place to assume that responsibility. Samuel's delay in coming was a test from God and Saul failed the test.

Before God can trust us with any type of leadership position, we must first learn to be led—not by the needs of men, but by the authority of God. If we cannot learn submission to authority, we will never be trusted with authority. Like Saul, we must learn to submit to the authority God has placed us under, even if we do not agree with the way they are doing things. Why? It is God who places men in positions of authority and He knows what He is doing with us. *"Everyone must submit himself to the governing authorities, for there is no authority except that which God has established" (Romans 13:1–2).*

David's Kingdom

"'Don't destroy him! Who can lay a hand on the Lord's anointed and be guiltless? As surely as the Lord lives,' he said, 'the Lord himself will strike him; either his time will come and he will die, or he will go into battle and perish. But the Lord forbid that I should lay a hand on the Lord's anointed' " (1 Samuel 26:9–11).

David knew that he would someday be ruler over the people of Israel, but he refused to be ruled by impatience even when he saw Saul's sin. He knew that God would establish his authority over the people and he did not want to receive it any other way. He also knew that as long as Saul was still alive, he was alive because God wanted him to be. He was determined to respect the authority that God had established, no matter what.

We must never rebel against the authority that God has established, even if that authority is negligent and our intentions to help God's people are the very best. We must never take any authority position that is not rightly established by God. Like David in 1 Samuel 26:11, we must respect the authority in the church as being God's anointed.

This is a lesson Saul refused to understand, and he paid dearly for his disobedience. He felt pressured (see 1 Samuel 13:12) by the people to disobey the Lord. David felt the same pressure from his men, but refused to disobey God (see 1 Samuel 26:8). It was David's kingdom that would endure, not Saul's. David's kingdom, through Christ, will endure for eternity because of his obedience. Saul's kingdom was short lived and is now just a story in history. *"But now your kingdom will not endure; the Lord has sought out a man after his own heart and appointed him leader of his people, because you have not kept the Lord's command"* *(1 Samuel 13:14).*

Saul's story can benefit us if we learn to wait in order to receive all that God has promised to us. We don't want to be a half-baked muffin! We want to be mature fruit! A part of waiting on the promises of God is submitting to the authorities that God has established in our lives. Our spiritual maturity is revealed through patience when dealing with the authority we are serving under.

Your Turn is Coming

If you truly love the Lord, you will submit to the authority He has established over you. Perhaps God is testing you to see if you will honor Him with a good attitude and praise Him in spite of your disappointment.

It could be that God has something much better for you than what you have hoped for. Our dreams are usually smaller than His. And in spite of the pain of disappointment He has to bring to us, He wants us to receive all that He has for us, not just what is easy for us to get. God can see your end from your beginning. And you can be confident that He knows what He is doing with you. Be patient and continue to trust Him; your turn is coming. Your destiny is on the horizon.

Don't lose heart! God loves you and He will do what He has promised He would . . . if you do not give up! We have nothing to gain by giving up!

I have to say, as a postscript to this message, that there are exceptions to this teaching. If you are in a truly abusive situation, you can, like David, flee for the sake of your own heart (see 1 Samuel 19:11). Forgive and release the offending authority for the pain they have caused you, and move on to whatever function God has established for you in your future.

God is well able to take care of any situation we leave in His hands. "Bless those who persecute you; bless and do not curse" (Romans 12:14). If we plead for God's mercy for them, then God will bless us!

~ *Chapter Twelve* ~

THE GATE
TO YOUR HEART

*Your Father in heaven wants you to be freed from the
wounds and disappointments of your past. He wants you
to be free to move on and fulfill your destiny in Him.*

If we can look at our hearts like a walled city, we
can see that the gate to that city is forgiveness.
Forgiveness is a powerful tool we can use to protect our
hearts against the enemy's attack. That is why Satan is always
eager to get us caught up into offenses that cause us to
become bitter.

Forgiveness is the very pinnacle of our faith in Jesus Christ.
And it is only through forgiveness that we can be truly free,
free to move forward, unchained from our past. *Forgiveness
is a gift to us, but it is a gift we must be equally willing to
give to others.*

Christ Forgave Us

His love for us is unconditional (see Lamentations 3:22–23), but his forgiveness is conditional (see Matthew 6:14–15). There are no exceptions to this rule. We can say that the offense that we feel in our heart is too great for us to forgive and let go of, but if we do not forgive we will be tortured by that misdeed for the rest of our lives. The person that wounded us continues to cause us pain each time we remember it, until we release that person to God and forgive. This is what Christ did for us and this is what He expects of us.

"For if you forgive men when they sin against you, your heavenly Father will also forgive you. But if you do not forgive men their sins, your Father will not forgive your sins" (Matthew 6:14–15).

He Expects the Same from Us

As Christ hung on the cross, He knew He was being brutally murdered by hatred. The hatred His murderers felt toward Him was indeed a great offense. They not only killed Him, but while He was hanging on the cross, beaten and humiliated, they continued to mock and insult Him (see Matthew 27:39). He was innocent and they were guilty. He was dying for them, and they mocked Him. Yet, enduring their torture, Jesus reached down into the reservoir of His strength and labored in His weakened condition to speak in their defense. He said, *"Father, forgive them, for they do not know what they are doing" (Luke 23:34).*

Their offense was great, but His forgiveness was greater. And He expects nothing less from us. He knew that the people who were hurting Him were not His enemies. He saw them as innocent victims who had been manipulated and used by His enemy, Satan. We need to see that behind every offense is our adversary, the devil. And *"He is seeking whom he may devour" (1 Peter 5:8)*. His target is not the person who offended you, but his target is actually you. His plan is to get you to hold onto the offense and open the doors of unforgiveness. When he does this, he can bring in a multitude of torturers to torture us with our past. Our past is allowed to take hold of our present, and the sinful behavior that we have been forgiven of and delivered from suddenly returns and tries to take root in our hearts.

The Bible, in Matthew 18, tells the story of *"a king who wanted to settle accounts with his servants."* He realized that one of his servants owed him ten thousand talents, so he had the man brought to him. He ordered that the man and his entire household should be sold to make payment for the debt. *"The servant fell on his knees before him. 'Be patient with me,' he begged, 'and I will pay back everything.' The servant's master took pity on him, canceled the debt and let him go" (Matthew 18:26–27)*.

As soon as the servant left his master, he found a man who owed him money and demanded payment of the debt. When the man could not pay and asked for mercy, the servant had him thrown into prison until the debt could be paid in full. Seeing the entire situation played out before them, the other servants in the household went to the king and told him what their fellow servant had done. *"Then the master called the servant in. 'You wicked servant,' he said, 'I canceled all that debt of yours because you begged me to. Shouldn't you have had mercy on your fellow servant?' In anger his master turned him over to the jailers to be tortured, until he should pay back all he owed" (Matthew 18:32–34).*

Free from Offense

When we choose not to forgive our brother, we open the door for our past to come back on us and torture us. There is a very painful side to unforgiveness that Satan does not like us to discuss. He wants to make you feel as though you will lose something by forgiving, but really *you have everything to gain and very little to lose.* You gain peace and joy, you lose the constant torture of remembering the offense. You gain the love and acceptance of your heavenly Father. You lose the chains of the fear of the incident recurring again. And you lose the agonizing entitlement of living in the cozy little jail cell of your past.

Suddenly you are free to move on. You only need to look back now to see how far you have come from the "old you" who kept every offense locked away in the treasure chest of your mind. The "old you" would pull out (at Satan's request) the woundings from your past, only to let them wound you again and again as you toss them around in your mind.

Dear ones, do not forget: You are a child of the King! Your heavenly Father rules the world and you are His heir. Your life belongs to Him, including the painful events of your past. He cares about you very much! He has provided a way out of the pain: you have only to open the locks and remove the chains . . . you have only to forgive.

Your Father in heaven wants you to be free from the offense; free to move on and fulfill your destiny in Him. As you move closer to fulfilling the call God has on your life, Satan will try to bring about circumstances that lead to unforgiveness. Disappoint him and forgive. Satan does not want you to fulfill your destiny, and he knows if he can get you into unforgiveness, you won't.

The very person who has offended you might be the one that God wants to use to release you into your destiny. Offense is the test of graduation. Forgiveness gives you an A+! Unforgiveness leaves you with a failing grade and you will repeat the course again and again until you have passed.

A Thorough Cleaning

"Bear with each other and forgive whatever grievances you may have against one another. Forgive as the Lord forgave you" (Colossians 3:13).

I went through a season in my life when God chose to do a thorough cleaning of my heart. I use the word *thorough*[1] because in Webster's Dictionary it means "complete and absolute." My heavenly Father laid the ax to the roots of unforgiveness in my heart and did not let up until the job was done. The word *thorough* is also appropriate because the root word of thorough is *rough,*[2] which in Webster's means "lacking comforts and conveniences." During this season in my life, God would not permit me to give any comfort or convenience to the sin of unforgiveness, no matter what the offense was or who had been used to offend me.

Often those closest to us will be the ones Satan uses to hurt us the most. It is easy to forgive the checkout lady at the grocery store who does not show us the proper respect. However, when those we love betray our trust, it is a much deeper wound and we need to be aggressive in our ongoing love for them. Our love for them will keep us from retaliation (see 1 Corinthians 13:5).

An Aggressive Defense

The enemy will seek to use our mouths to accuse the ones we love. We can stand in aggressive judgment toward them, with our finger wagging in their face and Satan's words of condemnation flying out of our mouths.

~ or ~

We can be used by God to aggressively defend those who have wronged us. Satan cannot condemn them if we, as the people they have offended, will stand in their defense.

When Aaron and Miriam spoke against their brother Moses, (see Numbers 12) for having a Cushite wife, the anger of the Lord burned against them. Miriam was struck with leprosy, but Moses interceded for her. *"So Moses cried out to the Lord, "O God, please heal her!" (Numbers 12:13).* Moses was not the one who sinned, but he is the one who cried out for God's forgiveness for his sister. He had the authority to intercede for her because he chose to forgive. If we love, we will not let Satan use us to condemn and accuse. We can be used by God to cover their sins. *Next time it might be our turn to be forgiven, and they may be used by God to defend us.*

In our home, when our children have a disagreement and one is clearly in the wrong, we often let the child who has been wronged choose "punishment" or "forgiveness" for the offending sibling. We remind them that next time it may be them in the hot seat, and they should choose for their brother or sister what punishment they would want chosen for themselves. Almost without exception, they choose forgiveness.

It is not always easy to forgive, but it is necessary; it is what Jesus is asking from us. He expects us to do as He Himself did. And yet, while they were killing Him, He was interceding for their pardon.

Pray this with me:

Dear Father,
Please uncover areas of unforgiveness in my heart and help me to release them to You. I choose to forgive those who have been used to wound me, because I want more of You.

Say out loud the names of those who have offended you. See them as victims of Satan's manipulation to hurt you, and release them by saying that you forgive them. Pray for them and bless them. Now, go on and fulfill your destiny!

[1] *thorough.* Webster's Seventh New Collegiate Dictionary
Copyright 1971 G. & C. Merriam Co.

[2] *rough.* Webster's Seventh New Collegiate Dictionary
Copyright 1971 G. & C. Merriam Co.

Chapter Thirteen

DAVID VS. ELIAB

As David went to the battlefield to see how he could help his brothers, he was appalled at Goliath's words against his people; he wanted to do something about it. But before David could fight against the giant, he had to overcome the accusations of his own brother Eliab.

"When Eliab, David's oldest brother, heard him speaking with the men, he burned with anger at him and asked, 'Why have you come down here? And with whom did you leave those few sheep in the desert? I know how conceited you are and how wicked your heart is; you came down only to watch the battle.'

" 'Now what have I done?' said David. 'Can't I even speak?' He then turned away to someone else and brought up the same matter" (1 Samuel 17:28–30).

W hen I read the title of this chapter to my son Cole, he very kindly informed me that I was incorrect. "No, Mom," he said, "it's David and Goliath!" We have all read or heard about the story of David killing the giant Goliath, but shortly before he killed the giant, his brother attacked him verbally. And before David could face off with Goliath, he had to overcome the heated accusation of his oldest brother Eliab.

David trusted in God's power, but his brother did not. Eliab thought the doubts he had about David's character were really wisdom. He misunderstood the accusations in his heart toward David to be a gift of discernment into his brother's life. He thought he understood his youngest brother. He had known David his whole life; he had probably helped to raise him, but could not see David's heart for what it was.

Eliab misinterpreted David's confidence in God to be arrogance and conceit. He thought David was just "talking big" for the boys, and it angered him. He had lived with David his whole life and just saw a little brother who was only good enough to tend the sheep in their father's pasture. Eliab did not know that while David was in the position of the lowly shepherd boy, God was training him to be a giant killer.

"But David said to Saul, 'Your servant has been keeping his father's sheep. When a lion or a bear came and carried off a sheep from the flock, I went after it, struck it and rescued the sheep from its mouth. When it turned on me, I seized it by its hair, struck it and killed it.

Your servant has killed both the lion and the bear; this uncircumcised Philistine will be like one of them, because he has defied the armies of the living God. The Lord who delivered me from the paw of the lion and the paw of the bear will deliver me from the hand of the Philistine' " (1 Samuel 17:34–37).

While no one was paying attention to David, God was training him to be a mighty man of faith—someone who would not rely on his own strength or wisdom, but on God's. God taught David how to fight *His* way and not the ways of other men. God taught David to use faith and a sling. When the fighting men of the day tried to train David to fight with armor and a sword, it was uncomfortable for him because he was not used to it (see 1 Samuel 17:39).

God Wants to Train Us

If we are willing, God himself will teach us and train us to walk in His ways. Many times God uses the experiences of other men to train us, but there comes a time when He desires to get one-on-one with us (see John 16:13). He desires to take us through our trials Himself, step by step, and the more we learn from Him, the greater our capacity to be taught by Him.

Eliab fashioned himself after the warriors of the day, and I am sure in their eyes he ranked very high. He was certain that he knew what it took to fight; he was sure David did not have what it took. After all, Eliab was the one that Samuel thought would be God's choice for the next king of Israel. The Lord told Samuel to disregard Eliab's appearance and his height, because He'd rejected him. *"The Lord does not look at the things man looks at. Man looks at the outward appearance, but the Lord looks after the heart" (1 Samuel 16:7).*

Eliab was furious with David for even thinking he, a shepherd, could fight the giant Goliath. Eliab thought David was conceited for talking with such great faith. Eliab reasoned that since he, the oldest and biggest of his brothers, would not even consider fighting with Goliath, how could his "baby brother" have the gall to think he could fight him. He was positive that David's talk was just conceit and that his intentions were wicked. Eliab was focusing on Goliath and thought he was too big for anyone to fight, but David's focus was on his God. Eliab thought that David was thinking too highly of himself, but actually it was Eliab who thought too little of God.

Turn Away from the Accuser

Have you ever been in David's position? Your intentions are honorable and your heart is pure, but those around you misinterpret your actions. They point at your confidence in God and assume it is pride, so they decide that they need to remind you of your smallness, as Eliab did when he reminded David he was only a shepherd. *"And with whom did you leave those few sheep in the desert?" (1 Samuel 17:29).*

People like Eliab allow their mouths to be used by doubt and unbelief. They will point out every reason why you could not possibly fulfill the call of God on your life. They are positive you could never have the things God has promised to you. Eliab felt he knew David, and he was sure there was nothing special about him. However, Eliab was not there in the fields with the sheep when God was fashioning David's heart after His own and building up his faith in Him.

It was at this time that David made one of the most important decisions of his life: he turned away from Eliab and started talking to someone else.

The enemy will find those people in our lives that regard us as inferior and unsuitable for ministry, and speak through them to devour our destiny. He will use them to point out our inadequacies and remind us of all the reasons why we could not possibly do anything of significance.

But God also has a voice! He can see into our future and the motives of our heart. We need to tune our ears into Him and He will encourage us to do all that He asks us to do. He wants us to break free from the person we have previously been and see ourselves walking in our destiny in God.

You are a Giant Killer

Beloved, God sees you as a giant killer. He sees you as victorious; He pushes you to try. Close your ears to the enemy's lies and see yourself as God sees you. *God wishes to use your uniqueness to enrich the body of Christ.*

God has been trying to convince you that your destiny is very great, indeed. But at the same time, those around you see you as insignificant. They may view you as anointed, but cannot possibly envision what God has planned for you. It simply is not possible for them to see your destiny. Don't expect them to; it is between you and God. He desires it to be that way until He releases you into your destiny in Him.

If David had listened to his brother Eliab, he would not have killed the giant, and he may never have become king. While anticipating the birth of our destiny, we must endeavor to turn away from the opinions of man and heed the voice of God. God promised David the crown of Israel, but he was virtually unknown until he fought and killed Goliath. It was through this step of faith that God made his name known. God gave him a platform by which he would eventually be made king and fulfill his destiny. Every step of faith and every act of obedience to God will get us one step closer to our destiny in Him. If David had not stepped out in faith here, he might not have sat on the throne of Israel.

What is the Goliath in your life today? What is God asking you to do? No matter what it is, be ready for the voice of the accuser to say you cannot do it. He wants to stop your destiny. Don't let him do it! When the enemy tries to discourage you, be encouraged by it. He would not waste his time trying to discourage you unless he actually thought you would fulfill your destiny in God.

Please pray this with me:

Dear Father, Help me to hear Your voice and not the voice of the accuser. Change my vision. Help me see myself the way You do. Allow me to see others in light of Your grace, and help me see Your destiny in people everywhere I look!

In the Waiting

~ Chapter Fourteen ~

WAITING FOR DESTINY

The longer we serve God, the deeper we trust that He will fulfill the promises He has made to us.

"Do I bring to the moment of birth and not give delivery?" says the Lord. "Do I close up the womb when I bring to delivery?" says God (Isaiah 66:9).

erhaps an even greater burden to us than that of giving birth is *waiting to give birth.* It seems as though the baby will never come. But it does! So it is with a spiritual birth. The Lord gives us a promise of something, and from that moment we long for its fulfillment. *The greatest test of our faith does not come with the delivery of the promise, but the greatest part of our energy is spent in waiting for the promise to come to pass.*

Unfortunately, we never know how long the wait will last; it always seems to take longer than we thought it would.

Abraham, I am sure, had no idea of how long he would have to wait to see the promise of his son Isaac come to pass. It is probably a good thing we do not know how long it will take, or we may not have the courage to wait for it.

Ishmael and Isaac

We risk giving birth to something not of God if we fail to wait for Him. Impatience has produced many immature ministries. Our impatience with God's ability to fulfill His promise can lead us to take matters into our own hands just like Abraham did.

Sarah spoke to Abraham and said, *"The Lord has kept me from having children, go, sleep with my maidservant; perhaps I can build a family through her" (Genesis 16:2).* Her words prompted Abraham to be impatient and produce an heir through Hagar, which later led to many problems for Isaac. We must guard ourselves from accepting less than the full measure of His promise. We must wait for our destiny to mature until it has developed properly and is ready for delivery (see Isaiah 66:9).

Hagar, Sarah's maidservant, was not to be the mother of Isaac. The promise would not come through her; it had to be fulfilled through Sarah in God's timing. There was nothing wrong with Hagar—she was young and fertile, and God did bless her son. But God likes a challenge. And He wanted to wait until it looked absolutely impossible for Sarah to bear a child; then He fulfilled His promise to Abraham and Sarah. God wanted to turn their impossible situation around for His glory; He wants to do the same for you.

He is worth waiting for because, as immature promises hinder the true promises of God, anything we try to push to make happen will always frustrate the fulfillment of our true calling. *If you bake your bread before it is fully risen, you will have tough bread.*

Mature Plants

When I was a little girl, my older brother planted a little garden in our back yard. I watched him as he worked in his garden. Being the typical younger sister, I bombarded him with all kinds of gardening questions. I could not understand the process of waiting for the seeds to grow. At five years old, I could not fathom the amount of time it took to grow carrots. Every day I would go out to his garden and check to see how his seeds were doing; for quite some time I walked away disappointed.

One day as I checked on his plants, I saw an amazing thing—little sprigs were sticking out of the ground. They were so cute, but all I could see were the tiny green tops. My older, wiser brother assured me that there were carrots growing, but we could not see them because they were under the ground. I believed my brother, but when his back was turned, I wanted to just make sure. So, I pulled up one of his plants. Indeed, there was a little carrot at the end of his sprig. I was so excited, I took it to Danny and showed him—"Danny, look at your carrot." He was somewhat dismayed by my actions and went in to tell our mother. I was so excited, but for some reason they were not.

Danny walked away with his baby carrot, back to his little plot. Mom proceeded to explain to me the time it takes to produce a mature carrot. When she told me that I had ruined the little carrot by pulling it prematurely, I felt bad. I went back to my brother and convinced him that we should try to replant the carrot, so we did. It grew a little more in the weeks to come, but it was never quite as large as the carrots that were left in the ground.

At the moment I pulled the carrot out of the ground, it was very small. It was runty and underdeveloped, but of course it was still in the process of growing and maturing. How absurd it would be to judge a carrot at this stage, and how mindless to judge people at a stage in their life when they are still growing and maturing.

Unfortunately, most people tend to judge others by specific moments in their lives instead of examining their lives as a whole. *We are not one moment; we are a lifetime.* God does not judge us moment by moment, but He observes our life as a whole. Someone who may be a factory worker right now could save millions in the future. The next great revivalist might be a housewife right now. The man in the gutter today could be in the pulpit tomorrow; the person in the mental ward today could be an evangelist tomorrow. With God, all things are possible.

Premature Responsibility Breeds Superficiality

We need to wait on God's perfect timing, and for Him to open doors for us. It will be much easier for us if we do. Being a Christian leader is a great responsibility in Christianity and should not be taken lightly. Ministry to others is a serious call. It can be very rewarding, but there is great heavenly accountability that goes with it. We should not seek out ministry until God has accomplished His work in us and until we have waited for His timing. We must let Him open doors for us and not try to pry them open for ourselves.

Trusting in God's Timing

We cannot rush the call of God on our lives, it will only lead to our ruin. I have had four children, and each time I was pregnant I had hoped to give birth much sooner than I did. I experienced what is called Braxton Hicks contractions, or false labor, with each baby. The contractions started at about seven months with the first baby and with each pregnancy after that they started sooner than the last. With my fourth child, they started at five months. When a woman starts having these type of contractions, it is supposed to mean that true labor is soon to come. There is no burden like that of being close to the end of your pregnancy, yet having to wait. Your load becomes very heavy and taxes your energy.

While expecting my third baby, I was past my due date and had gained 55 pounds. I desperately wanted to give birth to my baby. I tried everything I could think of to start my labor. I even took a rather large dose of castor oil. It did not start my labor—I just got very sick. Although it did not give me a baby, it did make my false labor increase. However, these type of contractions are of little value. They are superficial and produce pain, but no baby. Premature ministries are much like this. They are superficial, produce pain, and bear no fruit.

My time came when it was time, and no sooner. While we are waiting for our destiny to come to pass, none of our pushing produces anything that will make a difference. Our time comes when it is our time, and no sooner. Our ability to trust God and His timing will create a peace in our hearts that will carry us through to the culmination of our destiny. God impregnates us with a promise of our future and only He can give birth to the fulfillment of that promise. *Our own efforts to try and hurry things up will only cause us pain.*

"'Do I bring to the moment of birth and not give delivery?' says the Lord. 'Do I close up the womb when I bring to delivery?' says your God" (Isaiah 66:9).

We can trust God's timing. He loves us, and everything He does is for our good. God does not harvest seeds or seedlings; He harvests mature plants. Mature plants take time. God wants you and I to grow into big beautiful oak trees so He can show us off to the world.

Pray this with me:

Dear Father,
Make me the person You need me to be. Forgive me for trying to rush Your work in me. Grant me the grace I need to wait on You; give me a willing heart to sustain me.

~ Chapter Fifteen ~

HIDDEN, BUT NOT FORGOTTEN

He has you hidden for a purpose; you are His secret weapon!

"My frame was not hidden from you when I was made in the secret place" (Psalm 139:15).

Have you ever felt forgotten by God? Do you feel invisible? Does God seem to be blessing everyone except you? Do your expectations of God seem to meet with cold indifference from Him? If your answer is "yes," then rejoice, because you are at the edge of a miracle! You are on the verge of a breakthrough! The door to your destiny is about to swing open!

The most difficult time of any birth is the few moments right before you deliver your baby into the world. You are exhausted beyond what you can even endure . . . you cannot stand it anymore. You have pushed and pushed and have exhausted all your strength. You want to scream, "I can't do this . . . I can't!" BUT you must! It is at this moment that you must push the hardest and exert yourself the most. You are crying, "I can't," and everyone around you is yelling, "PUSH!"

Then, somewhere deep inside you, strength arises! You have a determination now, where a hopeless feeling used to dwell. Now you cry from the depths of your heart, "I can," and "I will!"

You are at the verge of a breakthrough and perhaps you are tired of believing, but only you can break through to your miracle. Only you can give birth to your destiny! Only you can fight through to your dream's fulfillment. Your God will give you His strength when you have none of your own. When you fall short, He will pick you up because, *"He gives strength to the weary and increases the power of the weak" (Isaiah 40:29).*

Hidden Miracles

I have felt this way. I have felt forgotten by God. I wondered if the promise would ever be fulfilled—if God would ever open the door. I had been teetering on the edge of a breakthrough for so long that I began to doubt. "Would it ever really happen?" "Maybe God has changed His mind?" I was tired of waiting, of praying, of hoping in faith! I felt like a butterfly in a cocoon, hidden and forgotten. During that time I wrote this poem:

Someday, I'll Fly

I've not been myself lately or for sometime for that matter.
I'm not sure who "myself" is anymore.
I feel like a caterpillar inside the cocoon.
I'm neither a butterfly nor a caterpillar anymore.
I'm not what I used to be nor am I what I'm going to be.
I cannot go back to what I was,
or what was familiar to me.

I can't rush forward and be what I have not yet become.
It's a miserable place to be.
It's much like a baby in the womb;
you have to wait it out and stay where you are.
I hope every day will bring the end;
I know God is almost done working.
I rejoice because the end is near,
but still the pain increases.

It's become too easy to not be anything, just a cocoon.
I want to give up, but You won't let me.
I'm not the caterpillar I used to be
and I'm not the butterfly I know I am becoming.

Becoming a butterfly is scary, painful and exhausting.
I guess I don't want to remain a nothing,
so I'll endure the torturous path out of this cocoon.
And I know, someday, I'll fly!

Years ago we lived in a house with dozens of trees around it. In the fall the trees were covered with cocoons. We would walk by them all the time without taking much notice of them. A miracle was taking place before us and we paid little attention to it. But in the fall, our trees were covered with hundreds of beautiful butterflies. Our children would run through the trees and the butterflies would all take flight. It was a glorious sight to see hundreds of butterflies fill the air, sunlight reflecting off their wings.

Caterpillars are ugly little things, but butterflies are gorgeous. God loves to make something beautiful out of something ugly. *God loves to take the ugly things of our past that Satan meant for our destruction, and turn them into a powerful weapon He can use for our construction. "And we know that in all things God works for the good of those who love him, who have been called according to his purpose" (Romans 8:28).*

Death Gives Birth to Life

God takes you through "ugly" situations only to turn you into something beautiful. The cross looked like the end of a dream to the disciples. They expected their Messiah to come, overthrow the Romans and establish His kingdom on this earth. The death of Jesus looked like the end of all their dreams.

Christ tried to warn the disciples of His impending death, but when He spoke of dying, Peter declared, "This shall not happen." Christ knew that this must happen. Like a seed planted in the ground must cease to be a seed in order to become a plant, He knew that His life on earth as it had been must end or He could not bring forth the gift of eternal life for those who would believe in Him.

"In a little while you will see me no more, and then after a little while you will see me, because I am going to the Father" (John 16:17).

His death gave birth to life! (see John 11:25)

The "cocoon" that you are in right now is the "death" that will give birth to your destiny. The painful situation you are enduring right now could be the launching pad for your future.

If you feel as though you are invisible, rejoice, because you are. *God has hidden you away to change you in secret, but soon He will pull you out like a secret weapon and show you off to the world.*

"Let your light so shine before men, that they may see your good deeds and praise your Father in heaven" (Matthew 5:16).

Your heavenly Father will declare, "Look at what My grace has done!" The world will praise Him because they can see what He has done in you. You are His trophy! His reward!

Some may argue then, that you have no right to be where God has placed you. But the voice of your accusers will not even reach your ears, because you *have* paid the price; you have endured and you have overcome.

And you *"will soar on wings like eagles" (Isaiah 40:31)* and, yes, you will fly!

This Could Be the Day

When the expected due date for each of my children neared, I would awaken each day with the expectancy that today could be the day that I would deliver this child. Each day I would think, "Today could be the day." I never thought to myself that it just could not happen today, because I knew my time *was* coming and that this day could be the day that I would give birth. As each day ended without seeing the birth of my baby, I would feel somewhat disappointed. But once again another morning would come and I would arise with hope from heaven, remembering that this day could be the day. And I was prepared to go at any time; I had my bags packed and gas in the car.

Each day that you serve God and wait on His timing for your destiny's fulfillment is one day closer to its birth. As you near your time of delivery, you feel in your spirit that the time is near. Perhaps today is the day! You look around you and see your Christian brothers and sisters receive the promises of God in their lives—you are happy for them. But when is it your turn? When will your destiny come forth in the way God promised it would? Each day we must prepare our hearts to believe that, "this could be the day He fulfills His promises to me," and then suddenly He does.

The longer you serve God, the deeper you will trust Him to bring the promise to pass for you. As you near the time of receiving the fulfillment of His call on your life, you can know that every day will bring you one day closer. Today could be the day you receive a great blessing from God. Today could hold the answer you have been waiting for.

Wait in faith through each day, as a woman waiting to give birth. God does not bring you to the time of birth just to stop the whole process. He did not bring you this far to leave you now. He will not forget you! It will happen! And remember that *"He who began a good work in you will be faithful to complete it" (Philippians 1:6).*

"God is not a man, that he should lie, or a son of man, that he should change his mind. Does he speak and then not act?" (Numbers 23:19).

If He has promised it, He will do it!

Say this with me:

God will do what He has promised. He has not forgotten me, for I am constantly in His thoughts. God is waiting to fulfill His Word through me. It will happen! This could be the day! God cannot lie; He will not change His mind. I choose to believe what God has told me and not the lies of fear and doubt.

Chapter Sixteen

IN THE WAITING

During the restless time of waiting for our destiny to come to pass, we can focus our energy on trusting God. We can trust Him to do BIG things through us. He wants us to trust Him for BIG things, but also for the small day-to-day provisions. We should not allow ourselves to become anxious while waiting, but appreciate the progress the Lord is making. Enjoy every little step and know that each one gets you closer to your destiny.

"Be still before the Lord and wait patiently for Him" (*Psalm 37:7*).

Being still and waiting on God is more than just not doing for ourselves what we are waiting for Him to do for us. We also need to find His rest for our hearts. Waiting on God is trusting in Him to answer us in His timing. Most importantly, *do not allow yourself to become frustrated and fretful.*

Delight in Him

"Refrain from anger and turn from wrath; do not fret—it only leads to evil" (Psalm 37:8). God equals the sin of fretting or worry to that of anger and wrath. Fretting is like having a loaded gun in your hands. At a moment of upset, you could unwittingly pull the trigger and release your frustration on others. Being fretful or frustrated can lead you to do things with an ambitious mindset.

Our hearts long for the promises that God has given us to be fulfilled in our lives. Longing in the flesh, without His peace, can keep us constantly trying to reason in our minds on how or when God will bring those promises to pass. We may end up wondering who God will use to bring us into our promised land. We lose our focus and begin to meet people, wondering what they can do for us, instead of what we can do to help them. We begin to take our focus off our Provider and focus on the people God could use to provide for us. This could lead to our caring more to please them than God. Waiting on God is easier when we keep our eyes on God.

"Delight yourself in the Lord and he will give you the desires of your heart. Commit your way to the Lord; trust in him and he will do this: He will make your righteousness shine like the dawn, the justice of your cause like the noonday sun" (Psalm 37:4–6).

When we are waiting on God, we can stand back away from our circumstances and watch God do for us that which we would never be able to do for ourselves. Understand that the greater our destiny, the longer the wait. We need to stop stressing ourselves and take our hands off the situation. Instead of wasting our strength treading water in the sea of frustration, we can delight ourselves in our God. Our soul is at rest no matter what our circumstances may be, when we delight in Him. When it appears as if things are not going our way, we can remain at peace when our eyes are on God and our trust is in Him.

Eve was tricked into disobeying God because Satan told her that God was withholding something from her (see Genesis 3:3). She was not completely trusting God to do what was best for her. It is important that we know without a doubt that God loves us—that He will do what is best for us. Even though we do not fully understand His methods, our trust in Him must be complete!

Let God Show Off

"And I have promised to bring you up out of your misery in Egypt into the land . . . a land flowing with milk and honey" (Exodus 3:17).

No one can bring us into our destiny in God except God. He does not need our help to fulfill the promises He has given to us. He is more than capable of doing it Himself. When we try to help Him, we only frustrate ourselves, and we usually mess things up and have to wait longer for the promise to be fulfilled. The best thing we can do is to commit our way to the Lord; trust in Him, and He will do whatever He has to do to fulfill the promise He made to you (see Psalm 37:5).

In First Kings, chapter 18, Elijah built an altar to God and asked for fire from heaven to consume the sacrifice. But before he did, he demanded that it be drenched with water three times. In front of all the people, the water filled the trench to prove whose God was tangible. He wanted to make sure that no one else but God would get the credit for the fire. Which is harder, sending down fire from heaven or sending down fire from heaven onto an altar that is drenched with water? If He can send down fire from heaven, then I am sure He is big enough to send the fire when the altar is wet. When we expect big things from Him, it pleases Him. When we try to make things easier for God, it shows we do not trust in His ability.

When God gives us a promise of something in our future, we should never get the idea that He expects us to execute it. All we need to do is accept it and follow His leading. We, like Elijah, need to let God show us His power as we relinquish control of the fulfillment of our destiny to Him.

If God has promised to do something for you, then it was His idea and not your own. You should not allow yourself to become anxious for the promise to come to pass, but *enjoy watching the progress God is making, each step bringing you nearer to your dream.*

Trusting Him for Daily Progress

When the children of Israel were in the desert, the Lord provided food for them every day. A daily portion of manna was given to them every morning. God wanted to develop a relationship of trust between His people and Himself, so He would not allow them to gather extra to reserve for themselves. He wanted them to trust Him for each day's provision.

"The Israelites did as they were told; some gathered much, some little. And when they measured it by the omer, he who gathered much did not have too much, and he who gathered little did not have too little. Each one gathered as much as he needed. Then Moses said to them, 'No one is to keep any of it until morning.' However, some of them paid no attention to Moses; they kept part of it until morning, but it was full of maggots and began to smell" (Exodus 16:17–20).

The children of Israel tried to store up manna for themselves; their objective was to have some left over for the next day. But God would not allow it, and the manna rotted. Why would they do this? Had not God promised there would always be enough for their daily needs? He had not failed them before, and He was not lying to them now. Some might assume that the Israelites took extra manna because they were selfish, but I think their problem was, in fact, fear. They had a difficult time trusting God.

Our instincts tell us to rely on ourselves; our own self-sufficiency can be the most difficult stronghold to tear down. In our society we give people medals for being self-reliant. In fact, self-reliance can be a virtue, except when it conflicts with our ability to trust in our Father's provision.

"Blessed is the man who makes the Lord his trust, who does not look to the proud, to those who turn aside to false gods" (Psalm 40:4).

It did not make sense to the Israelites not to gather extra manna for their families. They were, after all, in the desert and there is not much vegetation that flourishes there. They found food lying on the ground miraculously provided for them. A God that they could see manifest in a cloud provided it for them, but still they were unsure of His continued provision for them. They were told that it would be provided fresh for them every day, but fear took over their hearts and they attempted to provide for themselves.

Many Christians have made self-sufficiency an idol they worship. It is a religious spirit that tells them they have done so much and come so far. They are proud of all they have accomplished for God. It seems unholy to them not to be doing for the Lord, but we can do and do and do and do, and all we end up with is a lot of "doo doo" if we do not do it with God. God is not interested in what we can do for Him, but what we submit to Him. *No one can bring us into the promises He has for us, not even we ourselves.* And if we try to do it on our own, we wind up in a sea of frustration and impatience.

"Come to me all who are weary and burdened, and I will give you rest" (Matthew 11:28). Christ's message is simple: "Cease striving, turn to me, and I will give you complete peace." No matter what your circumstances are, God loves you. He wants to take your heavy load from you and

give you the peace that passes all understanding (Philippians 4:7).

Pray this with me:

Dearest Father,

Help me to cease striving, let go of my fretting, and trust completely in You. Remind me of Your goodness and Your grace so that I may know that all that You have for me will be good. Help me to trust You with all the promises You have made to me.

~ *Chapter Seventeen* ~

"SHE IS NOT DEAD, BUT ASLEEP!"

Does it look to you as if your dreams are dead? Does it look as if the promises of God will never happen for you? Then you need to rejoice, because God is not a liar. What He says will happen will come to pass!

"Don't be afraid; just believe" (Luke 8:50).

Your dreams are not dead, just asleep!

When Jairus, the synagogue ruler, and his wife were told that their daughter was dead in Luke, chapter 8, they were faced with this challenge: "Don't fear, just believe!" It was obvious to everyone present that their daughter, their only child, was indeed dead. At this devastating report, the Lord told them not to fear, just believe.

In spite of death, which seems very final, He challenged them to believe that she would "be healed."

He did not say she would be raised from the dead, but that she would be healed. He said "healed" because, to God, even death is not final. What they saw as final and hopeless, God saw as nothing. Nothing to fear. Nothing to panic over. Nothing! Even death is nothing to our God.

If you have been told by even the highest authority that your situation is hopeless, that your dream is dead, you need to rejoice. God's reality is much different from the world's and His is the only one that matters.

Jesus did not see their daughter as dead. That is why He said: *"Stop wailing . . . she is not dead, but asleep" (Luke 8:52)*. Many of you need to hear that. Your dreams are not dead, only asleep. You need only to believe, in spite of what your circumstances appear like. It may look as though you will never succeed, but our Lord is challenging you today. Do not give up, just believe. Trust Him in spite of all the wailing going on around you. You will see your miracle.

Hope On

There have been times in my life when disappointment has dealt a crushing blow to my faith. The pain was so great that I resisted Christ's urging to keep hoping. I wanted my hope to die. I did not want God to give me more faith to believe, just to have it crushed again.

However, it is hard to resist the Lord's urging to HOPE ON. Oh, how our Lord loves to test our faith this way. I wish He did not, but that is how our faith stretches. That is how we learn that He does not lie and that He is faithful to keep His promises.

The longer we believe His Word and have peace in spite of the wailing going on around us, the more solid our faith becomes. Please understand, we are not trusting in our faith to help us; that would be our works. No, our faith is in our Father who loves us and who will never let us down. Though we are bruised, He will never let us be crushed. If He has promised us something, then it was His idea to begin with. He is the one who has to finish the work He began in us.

"To him who is able to keep you from falling and to present you before His glorious presence without fault and with great joy—to the only God our Savior" (Jude 1:24).

If your dream seems dead or beyond hope, then be encouraged because you are on the verge of a miracle!

Shut Out the Wailers

"Meanwhile, all the people were wailing and mourning for her. 'Stop wailing,' Jesus said. 'She is not dead, but asleep.' They laughed at him, knowing that she was dead" (Luke 8:52–53).

When the enemy is laughing at you because of your faith, then sit back and breathe a sigh of relief, because your miracle is surely on its way. God will never let us be tested beyond

what we can stand. So, if people are harassing you because of
your faith in God, then know you are nearing the end. Be
encouraged by their doubting. Do not let it get you down. Help
is on the way!

*"When he arrived at the house of Jairus, he did not let
anyone go in with him except Peter, John and James, and
the child's father and mother. Meanwhile, all the people
were wailing and mourning for her" (Luke 8:51–52).*

We need to step away from the wailers. These are the
people who do not see God's reality, but only see in the
natural. They are not bad people, but they have not been
privileged to hear the conversations that the Lord has had with
you.

Jesus told Jairus alone that his daughter would be healed if
he would not fear but just trust in Him. When God speaks to
us about something, He tells us and no one else. It is our task
to believe Him, not the other people around us.

*"Faith is being sure of what we hope for and certain of
what we do not see" (Hebrews 11:1).*

Faith is seeing with your heart what your eyes cannot
possibly see! Do not blame the people who cannot see your
dream. Indeed, you need to love them. But there are certain
things that God shares with you that should stay between you
and Him. They are too precious and too personal to share (see
Matthew 7:6).

Come to Your Senses?

People who want to "bring us to our senses" are really very foolish, because the Bible says, *"We live by faith, not by sight,"* which is one of our senses *(2 Corinthians 5:7).* "Coming to our senses" means we live in the natural realm and not in the supernatural realm. They say, "If we cannot see it or hear it ourselves then we will not believe." That's anti-faith and anti-God, or should I say anti-Christ.

The wailers want so bad to help us. They want us to face reality. They say, "Come on, Jairus, anyone can see your daughter is dead." "Don't bother the teacher anymore" (see Luke 8:49). What did Jairus have to gain by giving up? A dead child? When your back is against the wall and your only hope is Jesus, then hope on!

You are in good hands, for God is well able to care for all that you have entrusted to Him. When He is in control of your life, you have nothing to fear. Just believe in Him and He will turn your darkness into light, your death into life.

"He holds victory in store for the upright, he is a shield to those whose walk is blameless, for he guards the course of the just and protects the way of his faithful ones" (Proverbs 2:7–8).

TRUE WISDOM IS—TRUSTING IN GOD! So, don't be afraid, just believe.

Pray this with me:

Dear Father,

Help me to trust You to guard and protect all that I have placed into Your care. Let me not comply with the voices of worry and fear. Help me to see life with my heart when all my eyes see is death. Thank you, Lord Jesus, for all that You have done for me and all that You will do for me in the future.

~ Chapter Eighteen ~

PRISONERS OF HOPE

There are times, while waiting for the birth of your destiny, that you feel as though you would like to give up hope, but God will not let you. It feels as though you are held captive by hope.

"Return to your fortress, O prisoners of hope; even now I announce that I will restore twice as much to you" (Zechariah 9:12).

 here are times during the development of your dream when your hope seems to have turned into a prison. You cannot make your dreams come true, and yet you find it impossible to stop believing in them. You cannot go forward any faster than God will let you, and you cannot return to where you once were before you became pregnant with the promise from God. God will not let you give up! During this time you might feel like saying, "Okay God, this is enough! I don't want to hope anymore! I am tired of being pregnant with this promise! I want out of this prison of hope!"

It is during this time that your dream feels so real to you, yet to others it does not. *The conflict between what you feel in the Spirit and what is evident in the natural grates at your soul.* You feel much like you are on a Ferris wheel. You have your up times when you can see your dream's fulfillment far into the future, but you also have your down time when you cannot see anything. You think to yourself, "Am I crazy to think that God would bless me?" The enemy comes in like a flood and you begin to doubt, causing anguish to your soul. *This is the time when God is doing His greatest work in you.*

It is Because He Loves You

You feel as though you are ready for your destiny, but once again God directs you back to the refinery for more tweaking. Oh, how weary you are of the awful refinery and that seemingly endless tweaking. "Okay, God, you can stop now," you scream, but He does not stop. You are caught in a prison of hope and He will not let you out until He is finished with what He began in you.

It is like a child who has a sliver. He does not like the pain the sliver causes him, but he hates the misery of having his sliver taken out. Removing the sliver is important, but he doesn't understand that. Even if he did, it is hard to keep still while it is being pulled out. Well, we all have spiritual slivers that we need God to take out, and sometimes it really hurts, especially when the sliver is way down deep in our heart.

This is when the refining process REALLY hurts, because He is getting down to the very core of your soul, to the deep regions of your heart. He is developing things in you that you did not know you lacked—things you did not even know you needed.

You think, "Okay, God, this is deep enough." But every builder knows you must dig down deep to lay a proper foundation first, before you start to establish the height of the structure. And the greater the height of the structure, the deeper the foundation must be.

It is God's great love for us that keeps us from entering our destiny until our foundation is secure. If He has held you back and you feel like a prisoner, He has done it out of love for you. He does not want to see all that He has worked to build in you crumble, because He did not take the time to develop a sure foundation. He loves you that much!

Even though it hurts you, He needs to hold you in the prison cell of hope until it is safe for you to come out. Even though you are sick and tired of hoping, of believing, of waiting, He will still make you hope, believe and wait even longer. And this can be the hardest thing He has asked you to do yet.

But when you feel like giving up, and yet continue to carry on, you begin to sense a strength rising in you that you did not know you possessed. And really, you did not possess it previously, because it was your reward for enduring this painful process. *It is a gift from God that the enemy cannot take away from you, because you have earned it.*

Held Captive by Hope

In the Word of God we can find many people who were held captive by hope; there are Moses, Joseph, and Abraham, to name a few. My favorite is David—his honesty in the face of misery draws my attention.

God had promised David that he would rule the kingdom of Israel, and Samuel had anointed him for it (see 1 Samuel 16:13). But after David had been anointed as king of all Israel, he had to go back to tending sheep. It was years before the promise came to pass for David, and he spent many of those years being chased by the man whose throne he would inherit. Back in the pasture on his father's farm, he did not envision himself hiding out in caves or pretending to be a madman in order to save his own life (see 1 Samuel 22:11). After all, God said he was going to be a king. A king does not have to do those things . . . does he?

In Psalm 119:82, David cried out to God in song and said, *"My eyes fail looking for your promise."* I understand the longing in his heart as he spoke those words. It feels, sometimes, as though the promise will never be fulfilled. But in fact, it was fulfilled for David, and it will be for you, too, *if you do not give up.*

Hopeless, No. Helpless, Yes!

Do you feel sometimes as though you are hopeless? Well, you are not without hope; you are not hopeless, but you are helpless. God has put you in a position of helplessness or complete dependency on Him, and you are helpless to help yourself. You struggle to gain some measure of control over your life, but your pride (that you did not even know you had) is being crushed during this helpless state, and *the only thing for you to do is to surrender and receive God's peace.* You may feel hopeless, but really it is the condition of helplessness that is causing you pain. *God wants you completely dependant on Him, and He will keep you a prisoner of hope until you are.*

Return to Your Fortress

Your fortress during this time is trusting in a loving God. Trust Him in spite of all the reasoning of your mind, in spite of the circumstances that surround you. You were content to give God control of your life until He decided to do something with your life you did not like. You were happy to surrender all to Him until He decided to give your promotion to someone else. You believe in His sovereignty, until His sovereign will conflicts with your will. Then you are sure He has made a mistake. You want to run from Him, but He is your refuge. How do you run from your refuge? How do you run from the only one who really loves you or understands you? The answer is . . . you don't. So, return, my friend, to your fortress and remain a prisoner until He is done with you; until *He* decides you are ready for all that He has for you.

What now feels like a prison cell to you, God sees as a fortress. And, of course, He is right. He loves you and if you give Him control of your life, He will guard it for you. Perhaps what feels to you like a prison cell may really be your place of safety and protection. David did not like being in a cave, but it saved him from King Saul. You may not like the circumstances you are in now, but do not run from them. They may be what is saving your life!

Double for Your Trouble

Why are we going through what we are going through? The second half of Zechariah 9:12 gives us the answer we are looking for. It says, *"Even now I announce that I will restore twice as much to you."*

God says, "Even now I announce to you that not only will I restore to you all that has been taken from you, but I will give you double for all the trouble you have endured." He says, "Don't stop now... keep trusting me, because I can see your future and it is very blessed. Keep walking with me and keep trusting in me and I will give you rest in the midst of the storm."

"Come to me all who are weary and burdened, and I will give you rest" (Matthew 11:28). When we have learned to "rest" in God in the midst of our storm, God is mightily blessed. It proves to Him that we trust in His goodness no matter what our circumstances appear like.

It pleases Him very much when we trust in Him, and when He is pleased He will burst forth blessings from heaven. He just cannot help Himself; He loves to bless those who trust in His goodness.

He, as He did for Israel in Zechariah 9:12, will stand up and announce to all that He is proud of you and intends to restore double to you for your continued trust in Him through all you have endured. And this is the beginning of your dreams coming true. Enjoy it, friend, because you have waded through the river of adversity and your heavenly Father is proud of you.

Return to your fortress, O prisoners of hope.

The Birth
of a Dream

~ Chapter Nineteen ~

THE POWER OF DEATH

There is a spiritual death that can take place in our lives which has great power to release life, much like that of the death of Jesus or the martyrdom of the saints. But this death takes place through persecution and rejection, pain and misunderstanding. It has the same death-like affect on our soul as does martyrdom and can work as a seed to release great blessing into our lives.

*C*hrist's crucifixion worked like an explosion to spread the message of salvation through grace, and when the enemy tried to stamp it out, it worked in reverse and spread like a wildfire. Satan thought that if he could kill the saints, he would kill the message, but it did not work that way. His method of annihilation only worked to increase its power, and Christianity spread like a fire!

There is great power that is released through persecution and martyrdom. The martyrdom of the first century church worked to fertilize the ground for the spreading of the gospel. God used the deaths of the saints as seeds to spread Christianity. Their lives brought many into the kingdom of God.

Our Father sent His Son into the world knowing He would be hated and killed. Christ, knowing that death was His destiny, trusted in God's plan and gave Himself to it. He gave up His right to defend Himself, embracing the cross and His Father's plan.

Death Before Expansion

In Mark 14, when the disciples and Jesus were celebrating the Passover at the Last Supper, Jesus prophesied to His friends that He would be broken. He took the bread and made it a spiritual representation of His own body, then broke it! Christ knew that it was only in the breaking that He would see salvation spread to the nations. He knew He would have to die to be *"poured out for many" (Mark 14:24).*

There is a spiritual principle that I call "death before expansion." We, our ministry, our church, our dreams must endure the breaking season before we can expand. In Mark 6, Jesus fed the five thousand with just five loaves of bread and two fish, but first He took the bread and broke it. In order for it to expand to feed the people, it had to be broken. After being broken, the bread not only fed a great multitude, but there were twelve baskets full of bread left over.

"They all ate and were satisfied, and the disciples picked up twelve basketfuls of broken pieces of bread and

fish. The number of the men who had eaten was five thousand" (Mark 6:42–44).

As kingdom children, we must endure a season of breaking—a season of dying. But when we have been broken, we will feed multitudes of people the bread of life that is released through that brokenness.

Pain . . . Plan . . . Purpose . . . Power!

"The stone the builders rejected has become the capstone" (Mark 12:10).

Many saints have experienced great persecution, not by the world but by the family of God . . . the church. They have been misunderstood, wounded and, in some cases, abused. It seemed as though Satan was having his way with them and that God had abandoned them.

Like Job, their friends have begun to wonder what great sin must be hidden inside their hearts. But, indeed, they are very close to God. So it is with many of you who have been wounded and rejected for the sake of Christ—your lives are lived in holy surrender to God. You are not being wounded because of your unholiness, but it is because there is so much good in you and because you *are bearing much fruit*!

God sees the good in you, but He wants to test it to make you even stronger. And instead of responding with a defensive attitude toward the wounds you have received, learn to lean into the knife of the Holy Spirit's pruning. Let the Lord have

His way in you. You will come back with a deeper appreciation for even those who have injured you.

As you look at the bigger picture of your life, you can see that it is the very pain or woundings that have become your greatest strengths. You minister now out of the areas of pain with power and authority. It is not just something you talk about, but you have lived it and it is a part of you. Your compassion is genuine and carries great power!

What you feared would kill you has actually become your platform for ministering to others. The pain of the mistreatment you endured was like a death to your soul. Why did God allow it? Because it was a part of His plan. He had a purpose for it and that purpose was to give you great power. Why has God allowed your circumstances to mount up against you? It is part of His plan for your life. Trust Him, there is a purpose for it.

The Death of a Dream

Francis Frangipane often says, "God and the devil want us to die, but for different reasons." We know why the enemy wants us dead, but why would God want to kill us? Of course, it is not an actual death, but a spiritual death which causes us to die to ourselves. We let go of what we hold so tightly; He takes away what we hold so dear only to give us something much greater in its place.

When we see the thing we love taken away, whether it is a ministry or a relationship, we find out how strong we are becoming and how much dying to self we have yet to do. Little by little, we learn to hold things more loosely and realize our only true need is Him. Our only true desire should be to do the will of the Father. As Jesus prayed to His Father before His arrest, in Matthew 26:39, *"My Father, if it is possible, may this cup be taken from me. Yet not as I will, but as you will,"* we should also pray.

You see, sometimes even our dreams can become too important to us; we become unbalanced. God has to let them die to show us what is important to Him. *Indeed, it is not what we do for Christ that pleases God, but who we become in Him.*

What may seem like the death of your dream right now could be the birth of something much greater—the heart of Christ dwelling richly in you. It is only through the death of your dream that you can fully enjoy its fulfillment. If you are willing to let it go, God will then release it to you.

Our true calling is to become one with Him in thought, word and deed. In other words, to become like Christ. If we do this, then God is pleased with us. We are not wasting our time as long as we are pursuing Christlikeness. Then we can minister to others in true power and authority, because it is not self doing it, but Christ through us.

Seeds

Our spiritual death through the pain of persecution or failure can become our seed. When planted in the ground, we see a great harvest.

"The hour has come for the Son of Man to be glorified. I tell you the truth, unless a kernel of wheat falls to the ground and dies, it remains only a single seed. But if it dies, it produces many seeds. The man who loves his life will lose it, while the man who hates his life in this world will keep it for eternal life" (John 12:23–25).

While predicting His death, Christ said it was His hour to be glorified. Why? I believe He knew it was only through His death that He could be glorified. The seed must first be planted and then the harvest will come. Do we, while planting a garden, keep our concentration on the seed? No! Even in the planting of the garden, we are not considering the seed as much as we are envisioning the plant that will grow from the seed. So too, as we endure spiritual death ourselves, we need not focus on the death, but on the life that will spring forth from it.

It is important to know that the cross is a part of the plan of God for our lives. Without it, God could not raise us up. It was in His last hours of freedom that Jesus spoke these heart-wrenching words: *"Now my heart is troubled, and what shall I say? Father, save me from this hour? No, it was for this very reason I came to this hour" (John 12:27).* In the same breath that Christ used to ask God to save Him from His destiny, He chose to submit to His destiny. He knew it was the will of His Father. It was through His death that He would bring forth new life!

~ Chapter Twenty ~

THOSE WHO HAVE COMPASSION

There are two kinds of shepherds in the body of Christ: those who have compassion and those who do not.

"By this all men will know that you are my disciples, if you love one another" (John 13:34).

The Lord said we would be known by our love! Our greatest witness to this world will not be our Christian bumper stickers, our big Bibles, or our spiritual intellect. All those things are wonderful indeed, but our greatest witness will be our LOVE. People are starving for love. The whole hippy movement was based on the desire to be loved. They wanted so much to fill their need for love with "free-love," but they were left feeling even emptier than they had previously felt. IF we, as the body of Christ, put our *love,* not our *religion*, on display in a great way, we would see the *world* come to know Christ.

The natural love of the human race is becoming colder, thereby giving us an even greater showcase for our God-given kind of love. *"See, darkness covers the earth and thick darkness is over the peoples, but the Lord rises upon you and his glory appears over you" (Isaiah 60:2).* This glory comes through an exhibition of love. That love proves our case for Jesus and will bring the nations to the light of the gospel (see Isaiah 60:3).

Ministry of Compassion

Jesus did not spend His time on earth just preaching great sermons, but He proved the gospel with acts of love. He truly cared for people, and was concerned for their well being. He did not just minister to their souls, but to their bodies as well (see Matthew 15:31). He cared that their practical needs were met (see Matthew 15:32). He proved His words with His acts of kindness to the people. Christ spent most of His time in ministry showing us how to love, and then He said, *"Love each other as I have loved you" (John 15:12).* He did not just tell us to love one other, but to love *as He* loved. And, *He laid His life down for others.*

"Greater love has no one than this, that he lay down his life for his friends" (John 15:13).

The Power to Disarm

Years ago, when my husband and I were youth pastors, one of our youth's parents came to me seething in anger. She was extremely upset and was quite forceful in her opinions. I listened to her complaints for some time, trying to reason with her. Then, I heard the Lord speak into my spirit, "Tell her you love her." As I did, she stopped short and began to cry. Her heated countenance melted into humble resignation.

What she really needed was to hear that we loved her. What was at the core of her complaints was the feeling that she and her children did not matter to us. When I assured her that they did, the lies of the enemy were disarmed.

Time and time again I have seen situations like this. People who have been offended turn into time bombs of emotions, and you are the target. It seems like the misunderstanding will never be resolved, but love is a powerful weapon and can disarm the bomb of offense. Love will peel off layers of hurt and woundedness. It is very powerful.

We can absorb their pain and lay down our own emotions and reasoning to free them from the coldness that has encroached on their heart. I have been truly amazed by the power of compassion.

I am convinced this power can cure the ills of our society and can empower the church of Jesus to be the light that Isaiah talked about in chapter 58, verse 10. *"If you spend yourself on behalf of the hungry and satisfy the needs of the oppressed, then your light will rise in the darkness and your night will become like the noonday."*

Two Different Spirits

First Kings, chapter three, tells us of two women who each had a baby. As they slept in the same house, one woman accidentally smothered her baby in her sleep. In the night, she woke up and found her baby had died. She decided to place her dead baby in bed with her friend and take the live baby for herself. In the morning when they awoke, the first woman realized what had happened. Their argument was taken before King Solomon who made a very wise ruling.

"Then the king said, 'Bring me a sword.' So they brought a sword for the king. He then gave an order: 'Cut the living child in two and give half to one and half to the other.'

"The woman whose son was alive was filled with compassion for her son and said to the king, 'Please, my lord, give her the living baby! Don't kill him!' But the other said, 'Neither I nor you shall have him. Cut him in two!'

"Then the king gave his ruling: 'Give the living baby to the first woman. Do not kill him; she is his mother' " (1 Kings 3:24–27).

The child's true mother was the one who had compassion on him. *She was known by her compassion.* We, in the same way, must be known for *our compassion, not our religion.* The world will not be looking for your religious badge that declares what denomination you are from, but they will receive your gospel on the basis of your love. They are looking for the love of God and they will not care what denomination you are from. Whether you are Baptist, Presbyterian, Catholic, Pentecostal or charismatic will not matter to them, and it does not matter to God, either. He will know you by your love.

Where are the true mothers and fathers of the faith? You know, the spiritual mothers and fathers who will care for the flock—who would give up their own lives, if necessary, to protect them?

Many of the spiritual leaders of today have gotten things turned around. They have the mindset that the flock was created to serve the shepherd. In actuality, the shepherding occupation was created to take care of the sheep. They are servants who are responsible for the well-being of the sheep. We, as Christian leaders, should see that we serve the body as though we were serving the Lord. The true shepherds will be known by their supernatural instincts to protect the sheep, not to control and manipulate them.

"I am the good Shepherd. The good Shepherd lays down his life for the sheep. The hired hand is not the shepherd who owns the sheep. So when he sees the wolf coming, he abandons the sheep and runs away. Then the wolf attacks the flock and scatters it" (John 10:11–12).

The woman who was willing to give up her baby just to see it live was rewarded by the king. She got her baby back. She had been moved by her compassion for her baby. And to spare his life, she gave him up. The false mother was willing to have the child destroyed, not allowing either of them to have him, to prove she was right. She was motivated by her love for herself; the life of the baby was insignificant to her. The true mother valued the life of the child more than she did her "rights" to the child.

If you desire to be a shepherd of any kind, you must know that your desire must produce an outward flow of compassion for those you lead. You will be known by your love, and the Lord will reward you by giving you many spiritual children. You do not need to have an official title given to you in order to shepherd God's people. You need only to love and respect them.

Pray this with me:

Dear Father,

More than any other gift that You give, Lord, I desire to love others. I ask now for the grace to love Your people, no matter their race, religion, social status or gender. Give me the gift of compassion, make me a true shepherd of Your people, pour Your love through me onto those around me.

Chapter Twenty-One

THE POWER OF BLESSING

A part of giving birth to your destiny is bringing life to the destiny of others.

"A word aptly spoken is like apples of gold in settings of silver" (Proverbs 25:11).

once knew a young girl who seemed to have a lot going for her, but consistently failed in many areas of her life. I could not understand why—she seemed to *choose* failure over a successful, happy life. She was beautiful, talented and intelligent, but it was obvious that she did not esteem herself. And she continually made bad choices.

For years I could not understand why she did not see her true value as a person—until I met her mother. Her mother saw her as the biggest failure ever born and told her so. She would vomit out her many objections about her daughter to anyone who would listen to her. With her daughter present she would declare to a roomful of people what a failure she was. It did not take great discernment to see why the girl struggled so. Why should she like herself when the woman who gave birth to her did not see any good in her.

As soon as she was old enough, this young girl ran away from her mother and began living with an older man. Unfortunately, her life was poisoned by the many seeds of destruction and self-hatred her mother had been planting in her since birth.

I believe this is what Proverbs 14:1 is talking about when it says, *"The wise woman builds her house, but with her own hands the foolish one tears hers down."* The girl's mother's physical house was in excellent condition, but the heritage she passed down to her child was devastating and led to her daughter living a very destructive lifestyle.

I have counseled with many people over the years who have struggled with terrible feelings of self-hatred. Usually, in the course of speaking with them, I discover that these feelings began when they were a child and many times originated with words spoken over them by a parent or other people in authority in their life.

The Tongue of the Wise

Years ago my husband and I attended a church where the pastor thought he could help his people by continually telling them what was wrong with them. He found fault with us and, of course, found fault with his entire congregation. It was no surprise to anyone that membership dwindled down to just a few people, and eventually he had to close the doors of his church entirely.

When we left that church, we were left with an ominous, oppressive sense of failure. It felt like a dagger had pierced our hearts. We struggled through life for a few years afterward, enduring one failure after another. We felt as if we were living under a curse—and, indeed, we were. The words of that pastor sowed seeds of destruction that acted as a curse over our lives.

Words are very powerful, especially when they are spoken by someone in authority over you. They can either be words of praise that breathe life into your life or words of criticism and judgment that erode away your sense of well being. *"The tongue has the power of life and death" (Proverbs 18:21).*

Once we realized that the effect of this pastor's words over our lives was acting as a curse against us, we sought out ways to release ourselves from its grip. We prayed many prayers, but still this feeling of failure hung on.

It was only when we were led to another man of God who was a true shepherd that the curse was at last broken. Without knowing any of the words that had been spoken over us, he spoke the exact opposite of what had been said. He made us believe in our destiny again. He spoke life into our spirits. And through the anointing that he carried, he broke off the words of failure and planted seeds of life and destiny in their place. The power of blessing brought life to our dreams, setting us free from the power of death and destruction. Satan could no longer keep us from our destiny in God. The power of blessing blasted the power of cursing.

"Reckless words pierce like a sword, but the tongue of the wise brings healing" (Proverbs 12:18).

When We Choose to Curse

God has a strange way of working the curses of others to our advantage. He uses them to refine us and shape us, and then He heals us through the power of His blessing.

Many people in the Bible lived what some would consider cursed lives for a period of time. David, for instance, was chased by King Saul, Joseph lived for fifteen years in prison for something he did not do, and Moses was chased into the desert by Pharaoh after living a life of luxury and ease. These are only a few examples.

Actually, God used this destructive period in their lives to shape and refine them. He promised them great blessings, but allowed them to go through the process of refining to prepare them for their destiny.

In order for Christ to fulfill His destiny, He had to suffer betrayal and be given over into the hands of his enemies. But He said in Luke 22:22, *"The son of man will go as it has been decreed, but woe to that man who betrays him."* We may have to endure a period of cursing for a time, but woe to the people who curse us.

In Psalm 109, David speaks about the man who cursed his life. *"He loved to pronounce a curse—may it come on him; he found no pleasure in blessing—may it be far from him. He wore cursing as his garment; it entered into his body like water, into his bones like oil" (vv. 17–18).*

When we choose to curse others and speak negatively of them, we are really only hurting ourselves. A part of birthing our own destiny is bringing life to the destiny of others. God wants to use us, but He wants to use us to bless others. Any jealousy we harbor towards the destiny of others will actually sabotage our own destiny in God.

Speaking Life

Our mouth is a very powerful weapon and we can either use it to bring a blessing or a curse onto others. When we speak negative words about people, those words act as a curse over them. Even if people never actually hear the words we speak about them, our words still have power and can cause them to experience oppressive heaviness. However, words of blessing can lift them up spiritually.

One day I was feeling exceptionally low. All of a sudden I had this wonderful feeling shoot through me. I felt a tremendous surge of pleasure and I knew everything would be all right. Later that day, a friend of mine called and said that she and her husband were talking about our family. She went on to tell me all the wonderful things they said about us. I asked her what time it was when they had this conversation and it coincided perfectly with the time I had experienced the surge of pleasure. That, my friends, is the power of blessing!

The Blessings of Heaven

One of our greatest weapons against the enemy is the words we speak. There is no question, then, as to why the enemy seeks to gain access to our words. He wants to use our mouths to destroy our own lives and the lives of others.

"The tongue also is a fire, a world of evil among the parts of the body. It corrupts the whole person, sets the whole course of his life on fire, and is itself set on fire by hell" (James 3:6). We can either use our mouths as a passageway for the fires of hell to gain access to earth, or use them to put out the fires of hell the enemy has lit in the hearts and minds of others.

You can be God's fire extinguisher. You can put out the flames of hell with the blessings of heaven. And wherever you go, you will be like a fountain of blessing that brings healing and life to the nations.

Instead of giving hell's fires access to the earth, you will bring to earth the very river of life that flows from the throne of God. People will be drawn to you like magnets because of the great power of grace and mercy that radiates from your spirit. And with only a few words you will destroy the curses of generations. This is the power of blessing. This is your destiny in God.

Please pray this with me:

Dear Father,

I repent of speaking negative words against others, and I ask You to stamp out those words and cause them to be ineffective. I receive Your forgiveness and mercy for my sin. Make me a fire extinguisher with power from heaven to destroy the seeds of destruction in the lives of those You love. Help me to walk in my own destiny . . . by blessing the destiny of others.

I bless you . . .

Lord, may this dear child of Yours walk in a manner worthy of the calling with which they have been called. May they indeed put out the fires of hell with the blessings of heaven.

~ Chapter Twenty-Two ~

GOD'S MERCIFUL JUDGMENTS

Many in the body of Christ today see God as a Father who only dishes out endless desserts to His children, with lots of hugs and kisses. But is that really a true picture of a loving Father?

*T*he Word of God clearly says, *"those he loves, he corrects" (Proverbs 3:12).* It is possible at times to lose sight of what true love looks like. God's discipline is as much an act of love as His blessings are. In fact, it is a blessing, because through discipline comes understanding.

Sometimes we act awful, but we are unable to see it. So, the Lord, in His kindness, shows us, through the hurtful actions of others, what we are doing to the people we injure. It is then that we are able to see how our behavior wounds those we love.

I have been through situations when my actions have wounded other people. Although I was able to see how my behavior hurt them, I was not really able to feel the pain I caused them. The Lord in His kindness then orchestrated different events and put me through the same hurtful situations as I had put others through. Now I was able to feel clearly how the other people felt. This was God's judgment on me because of my actions toward others; *it was His merciful judgment.*

God wants us to know how it feels when we hurt others so we will change, stopping any behavior that would harm His people. He uses painful situations to mold and shape us, and the best thing we can do is to let Him do it. *If we despise His correction, then we despise His love, because He disciplines those He loves.*

"I know, O Lord, that your laws are righteous, and in faithfulness you have afflicted me" (Psalm 119:75). It is not possible for our Lord to make mistakes in His judgments. They are always righteous! He allows us to be wounded out of His great faithfulness to us. He wants us to become all that He has created us to be and to be as loving and kind as He is. When we are hurt, our capacity to love increases.

The Gift of Understanding

"Your hands made me and formed me; give me understanding to learn your commands" (Psalm 119:73). God has made us and formed us, and He has no intention of leaving well enough alone. He will perfect us, and through His discipline we gain understanding.

Every parent knows that giving birth to a child is only the beginning of the work needed in order to prepare that child for adulthood. Parents may, over time, have to yell, pinch, pull, prod, or spank that child into understanding. They want their child to know and understand what is right. They will do whatever they need to do in order to turn their child in the direction of understanding.

God, in the same way, will not leave us or forsake us, but will do whatever it takes to perfect us. He will not leave us alone. He will discipline us, and that discipline is His way of giving us *the gift of understanding*.

The Gift of Failure

God will allow us to fail again and again so that we might come to know and understand what it takes to succeed. He lets us fail so as not to lose us to the sin of pride. He can teach us more through our failures and disappointments than we could have learned through a lifetime of successes.

Our failures can be the greatest gifts the Lord hands us. Of course, He does not *want* us to fail. That is not His desire. But if we need it, then He will allow it. God knew what passion would come out of the apostle Peter's failure. He denied Christ, but in light of that failure he became the first in history to win thousands to Christ in one single moment (see Acts 2:41). God also knew that the miracles pouring forth from Peter would be astonishing, so He prepared him ahead of time with failure, in the denial of the Christ whom he said he would die for (see Matthew 26:35 and 26:69–75).

God showed us the power of persistence in spite of failure in the life of Thomas Edison. When he created the light bulb, he had failed 1,073 times before he succeeded in lighting the whole world. He learned 1,073 times how NOT to make a light bulb. In the same way, we learn what pleases the Lord through trial and error, or should I say failure. If we do not ever fail in our pursuit of pleasing God, we become arrogant and cold-hearted, and don't please Him at all. We please Him more by enduring through our failures than without them.

Closed Doors, Open Windows

The Lord will close doors to us that we would very much like Him to open, so that He may open the windows of heaven and give us something much greater—Himself. It is so easy to go our own way at our own pace, and we get ahead of God. But even if what we are doing is right, *doing anything without God is wrong*. In His mercy, He closes doors of opportunity so that we might stop and deepen our intimacy with Him.

So often, we view the conclusion of the project we are currently working on as our goal. It may be *our* goal, but it is *not God's*. He desires, more than anything else, to develop our relationship with Him. That is His ultimate goal, and He will do whatever it takes to achieve it. That goal is much more important to Him than our successes.

In 1 Samuel 6, David failed at his first attempt to bring the ark of God into the city of Jerusalem, and it cost a man his life. Did this mean that God did not want the ark brought back into the city? After all, they were doing it for Him. They were trying to please God. They were doing a good thing, right? But David and his men were trying to bring the ark back *for* God and not *with* God. God wants a partner, not a slave. More than our acts of goodness for God, He wants a relationship with us. Wow! He loves us so much that our friendship with Him means more to Him than the "works" we do for Him. That is incredible love!

Obedience, Not Sacrifice

In Genesis, chapter 4, why was Cain's sacrifice not accepted but Abel's was? Cain failed to work *with* God, doing what God wanted him to do. He wanted to worship God in his own way by bringing his own sacrifice instead of what was required. But his *obedience* was the worship that God wanted.

God did not need more beef (see Psalm 50:9). He wasn't hungry (see Psalm 50:12–13). His goal was not to get more beef or grain, but to determine Cain's love for Him shown through obedience. Sometimes our pride leads us to give extravagant gifts to God that *we* have worked very hard on; Cain wanted to show God what *he* had been working on.

David said in Psalm 51:16–17, *"You do not delight in sacrifice, or I would bring it; you do not take pleasure in burnt offerings. The sacrifices of God are a broken spirit; a broken spirit and a contrite heart, O God, you will not despise."*

If God's discipline produces a broken spirit, then we are indeed blessed, because, *"The Lord is close to the broken-*

hearted and saves those who are crushed in spirit" (Psalm 34:18). God cannot resist us when our hearts are crushed, much like a mother who has punished her child's stubborn behavior and finds, because of her discipline, his rebellion has melted away to reveal gentle submission.

Discipline Brings Understanding

"Your hands made me and formed me; give me understanding to learn your commands" (Psalm 119:73). The Lord has promised you that He will never leave you or forsake you (see Joshua 1:5). You can take great comfort in this Scripture. But it also means that God will not leave you in the foolish condition He found you. He will not forsake the work He began in you. He wants, more than anything else, for you to become the person He has destined you to be. This is His goal and this is His joy. He delights in every aspect of your life. He desires to perfect all areas of your heart, not just the parts and pieces you desire to give Him. *"My son, do not despise the Lord's discipline and do not resent his rebuke, because the Lord disciplines those he loves, as a father the son he delights in" (Proverbs 3:11).*

And *"Whosoever loves discipline loves knowledge, but he who hates correction is stupid" (Proverbs 12:1).* Ouch! Whoever "hates" correction is stupid? You mean, God, that we have to love correction? Oh, boy! Do we have a ways to go yet? I guess we can start with this: It is only through the Lord's discipline that we can gain understanding. We need to see His mercy at work in our failures as well as in His judgments and correction. We surrender ourselves to the process of refinement, trusting that it is necessary for our own good. I guess we should stop feeling sorry for ourselves for the past and use the past to grow in grace so we can get to the good stuff.

Amen?

Pray this with me:

Oh God, help me to grow through Your discipline and not to despise it. May Your discipline have its perfect way in me, and may I love it.
Amen.

Unfolding Destiny

Chapter Twenty-Three

THE HOUR OF DIVINE REVERSALS

The time for the Esther generation has come!

"Vashti is never again to enter the presence of King Xerses. Also let the king give her royal position to someone else who is better than she" (Esther 1:19).

*I*f someone had prophesied to Esther that she would save the Jewish race, she might have laughed, but that is exactly what she did. In a mysterious change of events that only heaven could arrange, Esther's life was suddenly and divinely transformed. One moment she was just a woman without any authority to speak of, the next she was queen.

The book of Esther is a prophetic representation of what God is doing in this last hour. He is removing those in positions of authority who have not received His lordship and is giving their positions to those who will obey Him (see Esther 1:19)—to people who will fear and reverence Him, to people who will obey Him. God is looking for people who will not be corrupted by power, but who will see themselves as servants of the Most High even while they are being served.

Vashti's Disobedience

Queen Vashti represents the rebellious Christian who will not submit to the authority of Christ. Christ has given them their places of authority, but soon pride sets in and they begin to think more of themselves than they ought to. They forget they have only been given their position of authority to serve the Most High. They, like Vashti, refuse to obey the King.

"She has not obeyed the command of King Xerxes that the eunuchs have taken to her" (Esther 1:15).

Vashti's disobedience led the king to remove her as queen, and the entire kingdom began looking for her replacement. The king could not leave her in power even though he loved her, because if disobedience is not dealt with it could spread. And then, *"There will be no end of disrespect and discord" (Esther 1:18).*

The Lord our King will deal with us much in the same way. He gives us time to repent, but if we remain disobedient, He has to replace us, or our rebellion might spread.

Esther's Hour

We are in the last hour and the Lord cannot tolerate the disobedience that He once did. He is looking for a people who will give Him the respect He deserves. He is looking for a people who will obey! Our obedience to Him proves our love for Him. When He finds such a one, like Esther, He will miraculously move them into a position of authority. He knows that He can trust them to do whatever He asks.

Esther had seen her fair share of loss. She had lost her parents at a young age. Her older cousin, Mordecai, who treated her as his own daughter, took her in. She seemed to have been kept by the hand of God until the time He needed her. She was beautiful but insignificant. She went unnoticed until God moved her to her destined position as queen. Suddenly and unexpectedly, her life changed.

Esther was humble and obedient. She was told she could have anything she wanted, but took only what was given to her. Even after being crowned queen she continued to follow Mordecai's instructions, as she had always done.

God gave her favor, not only with the king, but also with others in whose care she was placed. She was the favorite of Hegai, the eunuch in charge of all the virgins brought to the palace. He chose to give Esther the best the palace had to offer.

"The girl pleased him and won his favor. Immediately he provided her with her beauty treatments and special food. He assigned to her seven maids selected from the

king's palace and moved her and her maids into the best place in the harem" (Esther 2:9).

The king was attracted to Esther more than to any of the other women, *"so he set a royal crown on her head and made her queen instead of Vashti"(Esther 2:17).* He gave a feast and declared a day of celebration in her honor—he called it "Esther's banquet." He "distributed gifts with royal liberality."

More Honor

If this were the end of the story it would be a very good book, but God had more in store for Esther. More honor, more authority, and even more prosperity. God was putting her in a position of authority because He needed her to save her people. Because of her humility and obedience to Him, God knew He could trust her.

God wants to do the same for us! He wishes to put us into positions of authority and influence. He wants to bless us with unreasonable favor. He wants to give us *"the best place" (Esther 2:9).* The places others have longed for, He will give to us. Through unexpected, unexplainable circumstances, He will move us from the "kitchen" to the "palace." As servants of God, we will be given favor even with world leaders. We will be given wealth and fine things, but we must remember: it all belongs to Him.

God wants to bless us for a purpose, a kingdom purpose. He wants to lift us up to places of influence and prosperity, but it is not just to bless our bank accounts. It is because He knows that, like Esther, we have been positioned for a purpose and when He commands us, we must obey Him.

After fasting with her people for three days, Esther approached the king and asked him to rescue her and her people from Haman's declaration of destruction. Esther risked not only her position as queen and all the blessing and honor it brought to her, but she risked her life to obey God. Esther knew that nothing God had given her really belonged to her. She offered it all freely back to him, even her own life, and said, *"if I perish, I perish" (Esther 4:16)*. She knew that Mordecai was correct when he assumed that she might have come to her royal position *"for such a time as this" (Esther 4:14)*.

God is looking for a people He can bless: *A people who will have everything and own nothing*. In this last hour, God is looking for a people who will love Him more than their own lives. He wants a people who love Him more than their possessions, who love Him more than their positions.

Satan is looking for a "Haman" who, because of pride, can be used to destroy the children of the Most High. But have no fear! God is looking for a people like Esther who will serve Him in humility and obey even if He asks them to risk their lives. He looks for a people who will, in spite of fear, not shrink back from their call, and trust their God for provision and protection.

"They overcame him by the blood of the Lamb and by the word of their testimony; they did not love their lives so much as to shrink from death" (Revelation 12:11).

Will you be one of these great saints who, in spite of prosperity and position, live only for the Lamb? Will you gladly give all you've been blessed with, even your own life?

The Time is Now

Vashti thought she was important because she had acquired wealth and position. She did not realize how futile those accomplishments were. She lived for herself and for the moment, much like the church in Laodicea. To it Christ said, *"You are neither cold nor hot. I wish you were either one or the other! So, because you are lukewarm—neither hot nor cold—I am about to spit you out of my mouth" (Revelation 3:15–16).*

The Lord says, "I am about to fulfill this Scripture; the time is now!" Now, you must choose the temperature of your love for Him. Will you be hot or will you be cold? Will you be a part of the Esther generation or of Vashti's? Vashti at one time loved her king, but because of her lack of passion and respect for him, she was thrown out of his presence.

Jesus is standing at the door of your heart right now, *"If anyone hears my voice and opens the door, I will come in and eat with him, and he with me" (Revelation 3:20).* Open up your heart to him and do not turn your destiny away. Do not be like Vashti, who did not know she would be thrown out of the king's presence because her love for him had become unenthusiastic.

"You say, 'I am rich; I have acquired wealth and do not need a thing.' But you do not realize that you are wretched, pitiful, poor, blind and naked" (Revelation 3:17).

A reversal is coming and we must repent of our lukewarmness and choose to buy from Christ gold refined in the fire so we can become truly rich! He is offering you true wealth. Your obedience to Him can no longer be halfway; He wants all of you or none. Again I ask you: Will you be a part of the Esther generation? If your answer is yes, get down on your floor right now. Kneel, and give Him your future.

Pray with me:

Dear Father,
I want to be a saint You can trust. In love and sincerity I give You my life to do with as You will. I am Yours, use me. Do anything that you have to do to refine me, and discipline me so that I can overcome the areas of luke-warmness in my heart. Clothe me with white garments, and give me, in return for my life, refined gold.

~ Chapter Twenty-Four ~

I AM WITH YOU

When the Lord begins to fulfill your destiny, the enemy will try and destroy it in its infancy.

"The dragon stood in front of the woman who was about to give birth, so he might devour her child" (Revelation 12:4).

We have talked about the similarities between giving birth to a child in the natural and giving birth to our destiny in the spirit realm. There is a time of conception, of waiting, of labor and there is also delivery. After we give birth to the promises of God for our lives, our destiny is in its most vulnerable state. It is then that the enemy will try to gain access to it in order to devour it.

At the moment our destiny is birthed, it is in its most helpless state. We can do nothing for ourselves, and if we were left alone, we would surely be destroyed. Just like a newborn child needs tender care to keep it healthy and happy, we need our Lord more now than ever. So, why would the Lord allow in His plan for us to be tested at such a vulnerable time? It is because at this stage He is able, because of our lack of pride, to help us the most. And we are in desperate need of His help. We don't know what we are doing and He likes it that way. At this point, God expects us to place our trust and reliance in Him. He is in charge; with every trial we grow stronger and stronger in Him. We are driven more and more into God. We know our need is great. We see now how vulnerable we are and how much we need to obey Him.

The Christ child was no exception. Yes, He was very special, but this little baby could not save the world even though that was His destiny. He could not even change His own diaper. However, three kings, many shepherds, and a host of angels honored Him as the Savior of the human race. Herod feared Him and realized there was no better time to try and destroy Him than to kill the Savior while He was a helpless child. Herod killed hundreds or perhaps thousands of babies while he was trying to destroy Jesus. Even with all his horrendous efforts to kill Jesus and stop the promise from coming to pass . . . he failed. He did not destroy Him because God saved Him again and again.

This is one thing that we know to be true; when the Lord begins to fulfill a promise, the enemy will try to destroy it in its infancy. When your destiny is birthed, all hell seems to come against it. Your destiny, even in its infancy, is a prime target for the enemy. He wants to destroy it while it is small and seemingly helpless . . . we should expect this.

We should not fear this attack, because it is indeed a part of the process of birth. You may not look very threatening to the enemy now; you may even feel like a failure. However, Satan, like Herod, knows your future and is terrified of you.

God's Protection

I believe that the vision of the dragon waiting for the woman to give birth in Revelation 12:4 is a prophetic picture of Christ, but quite often in Scripture there is more than one meaning to a passage. I believe this Scripture is also a picture of the enemy's tactics against our future in Christ. We know he does not play fair, that he will strike us at our weakest. He did not play fair with Jesus and he will not play fair with us.

"Do not fear, for I have redeemed you; I have called you by name; you are Mine! When you pass through the waters, I will be with you" (Isaiah 43:1–2). When we walk through the waters of persecution, we see God clearer and experience a greater measure of His power to protect us. We do not grow fearful because of these circumstances, but we grow in the confidence we have in our Lord.

Christ's defeat, after He was born, seemed inevitable. He was the Savior, but He was just a helpless baby . . . or was He? Don't forget the God of destiny. The God of the whole universe is watching out for you. And no matter what comes upon you, you can be assured that you will see the dawn of destiny's light. You have nothing to fear because God is with you. *"I am with you and will watch over you wherever you go" (Genesis 28:15).*

In spite of all that life throws at you, you know that you are in the arms of a gentle heavenly Father, and every battle you endure He will use to strengthen you. Through every trial, you gain knowledge. In every test, whether you pass or fail, you become more aware of God's mercy and grace. It is God's desire that you possess more of His Son's character through every trial you endure.

Our Destiny

"She was pregnant and cried out in pain as she was about to give birth" (Revelation 12:2).

This woman's destiny was to give birth to a child. She was in great pain, but her pain was a part of the plan. It had a purpose! How often do we want the pain to be over with. It hurts and we do not understand it, but it is a part of God's plan for us and we must trust Him. It produces a power that can be gained by nothing else.

Do not despair, my child, He will carry you through every valley and to every mountaintop. Don't waste your energy or your heart trying to rush through or away from your pain. Immerse yourself in it and work with it to produce the purpose and power God intends.

When the Lord Builds the House

"For he spoke, and it came to be; he commanded, and it stood firm" (Psalm 33:9).

God set into motion the days that we live in. He spoke and separated the light from the darkness. The light He called day and the darkness night. Every morning when we awake and the sun rises with us, we experience God's faithfulness to the plans He has spoken into being. It does not matter if we make mistakes; God is faithful to defend what He has set in place. *"The Lord foils the plans of the nations; he thwarts the purposes of the peoples. But the plans of the Lord stand firm forever, the purposes of his heart through all generations" (Psalm 33:10–11).* When the Lord has set you in place, you will stand firm. He will keep you!

"Unless the Lord builds the house, its builders labor in vain. Unless the Lord watches over the city, the watchman stands guard in vain" (Psalm 127:1).

Only God can keep you. If He has set you into place, He will be faithful to keep you. What God has established, He is faithful to protect. Your destiny is in God's hands and He will not fail you!

The only destiny worth having is the one God has planned for you. The only house that is of any value to you is the house that God has built for you.

Dearest Father,
I bless what You are building in this dear child of Yours.
I pray now that You would complete and defend what You have created in their heart. May Your unfailing love rest upon this one, even as they put their hope in You. Amen.

Chapter Twenty-Five

HOPE IN LOVE

God's passion is seeing you walk in all that He has for you.

"His pleasure is not in the strength of the horse, nor his delight in the legs of a man; the Lord delights in those who fear him, who put their hope in his unfailing love" (Psalm 147:10–11).

ⓘ know that sometimes it is very difficult to trust in God while waiting for the development of your destiny. *But we hope not in hope itself; we put our hope in God's unfailing love for us.* And His love for us is strong enough to sink our hope into, because in the vast creation of the whole universe, His delight . . . is in you.

Our Father's Pleasure

I love the way David expresses himself in Psalm 147. He says our Father's pleasure is not in the great strength of a horse or the strength in the legs of a man. Of course, He made these things and is pleased with them, but they are not what He delights in. Yes, God has the stars, moon and sun that He could delight in, but they do not hold any great pleasure for Him. What God is passionate about is not the world He has created. They were only gifts He made for the one He loves to enjoy. What He delights in, my friend, is YOU.

You are the apple of God's eye. You are what He is passionate about. Not the great white whale, the Hawaiian Islands or the Rocky Mountains, but you. And when you turn your gaze toward Him, His heart skips a beat. You are what He loves—the great passion He delights in. And those who hope in His love for them, He will not deny.

Your Hope is Your Worship

Your hope in God is the greatest honor and praise that you could give Him; it delights Him. You could not show your love for God any greater than by hoping in His goodness . . . trusting in His love. God wants for you to really know that He is good. And when you do, He will stop at nothing to bless you.

Unfailing Love

It is difficult to wait and hope, yes. But let's think about what we are hoping in . . . His unfailing love. God's love is not fickle like man's love. No, Psalm 145:8 says, *"The Lord is gracious and compassionate, slow to anger and rich in love."* His love is unconditional. We think we understand His love, but really we do not. If we did, we would not treat others the way that we do.

God does not stop loving us when we fail. He does not want us to fail, because He knows it will hurt us, but He definitely does not stop loving us. His red-hot love for us does not cool either. He loves us as much today as He will ever love us in our lifetime. He knew exactly what He could expect from us before He first chose us, and He chose us anyway.

Seasons Change

Flowers do not bloom year round, but do we lose faith in them because they stop blooming for a time? No, because we understand the different seasons they go through. And God understands that we go through different seasons and changes. Sometimes we bloom and sometimes we don't.

God loves us and appreciates us just as much when we are not in bloom, because He knows all and sees all. You may be going through a difficult time right now, but God looks ten years into your future and smiles. He never panics when we make mistakes, He just uses our mistakes for His glory. That is the love we hope in.

There is a time when every pot is a lump of clay, but God looks at that lump of clay and sees a beautiful pot!

"For I know the plans I have for you," declares the Lord, "plans to prosper you and not to harm you, plans to give you a future and a hope" (Jeremiah 29:11).

No matter what you are going through right now, God's plans for you remain the same. When a little child is just learning to walk and happens to fall down, his parents do not become angry with him. They do not get upset with him because he falls. Instead, they rejoice in the fact that he is *trying* to walk. They do not regard it as a failure, but enjoy watching him learn. And your Father in heaven sees you exactly the same way.

God never gives up . . . no matter how many times we fail, His plans for us never change. We may have to endure a time of chastisement or setback, but His plans for us never change. He will never give up on us, either, because He sees the finished product.

The Least of the Least

In Judges 6, the Israelites were crying out to God to save them from the Midianites, Amalekites and other eastern countries who raided their land and left no living thing for Israel to survive on. They were desperate and prayed to God for help. The help God sent was Gideon. God had great plans for Gideon, but Gideon did not see it in himself. There was greatness in him, but he felt inadequate for the job and even argued with God about choosing him to lead Israel (v 15).

God spoke to Gideon and told him to *"go in the strength you have."* When Gideon argued and asked, *"How can I save Israel?"* God's answer was simple. He said, *"I will be with you" (Judges 6:16).* The answer to all of Gideon's inadequacies was the same, *"I will be with you."* Gideon was left with only one answer and that was to hope in God's unfailing love for him; that was enough.

Even though Gideon was the least of the least of the tribes of Israel (see Judges 6:15), God used him to change a nation. And He will use you in the same way, because He delights in those who put their hope in His unfailing love (see Psalm 147:11). You may feel like nothing special right now, but God sees greatness in you. He sees a mighty warrior!

There is Greatness in You

As with Gideon, God sees greatness in you. For much of your life, that greatness may be kept a secret, but it is still in you. God is faithfully preparing you for your destiny. He is molding you into the person He desires you to be: *The kind of person who is bold enough to know that there is greatness inside of them, but humble enough to know where that greatness comes from.*

It can be very troubling for you to believe in your destiny when you feel inadequate, but let me assure you . . . there is greatness in you. And you will, like Gideon, fulfill your destiny in God. He will have His way with you, if you place your hope in His unfailing love. *Put your hope in the fact that you know He loves you and that He desperately wants what is best for you.* He wants to make your dreams come true. He wants to bless you more than you want to be blessed.

Hope in God . . . hope in love. Let go of fear, for your destiny is in good hands. He is able to do above and beyond all you could ask or hope or dream (see Ephesians 3:20). He is driven by love. His passion is *you* and seeing you walk in all that He has for you, and He will do whatever it takes to get

192 / The Birth of Your Destiny

you there. After all, it was His idea to call you in the first place and He will finish what He began in you.

You are on the adventure of your life, so remember to enjoy the process. Enjoy every aspect of your journey with your heavenly Father who loves you. And praise God with your smile. At a time like this, the best thing to do is smile, because you are in God's hands.

"The Lord will fulfill his purpose for me; your love O Lord, endures forever—do not abandon the works of your hands" (Psalm 138:8).

Pray this with me:

Dear Father,
Help me to see Your love for me and help me to hold on to Your love. I want to see myself the way that You see me. Help me to trust, believe and hope.

My prayer for you:

Dear Father,
I ask You to bless this dear saint with everything they will need to see the birth of their destiny come to pass. Anoint them for Your purposes and help them to succeed. Help them to know of Your great love for them, and help them to trust in that love. Please send people to them who will represent Your heart toward them.

~ Chapter Twenty-Six ~

UNFOLDING DESTINY

ou are a child of destiny and God will not let go of your life. Indeed, the promises of God are unfolding before you everyday. God has great plans and dreams for your life, and He wants you to receive all that He has for you. But more than anything He wants you to receive Him.

In Webster's Dictionary *destiny*[1] is described as a "predetermined course of events." Your destiny is an unfolding process, not any one single event. You are on an amazing journey that will lead you to fulfill the call God has on your life, indeed, you are on an adventure with God. And it will inevitably lead you closer to God while you continually step toward the fulfillment of His plan for your life. The pursuit of your destiny is the vehicle that God uses to bring you closer to Himself. He is not a tool to get you to your destiny, but your destiny will bring you closer to Him.

So, if you are asking yourself, "what is my destiny?" —the very essence of your destiny is to walk with God. And out of that walk will flow everything you will need to fulfill the plans that God has for your life.

The journey to the fulfillment of your destiny will also bring you to the prize. He is your prize; your reward. And if you did not have a prize at the end of your journey, then what is the use of the journey?

Every step of your journey is important and each step will take you closer to God. Your journey is the agent that God uses to bring you to Himself. And the relationship that develops through the course of the journey is the prize—oh, what a prize He is! In the words of the apostle Paul, *"I consider everything a loss compared to the surpassing greatness of knowing Christ Jesus my Lord" (Philippians 3:8).*

Press On

Paul said to the Philippians, *"Not that I have already obtained all this, or have already been made perfect, but I press on to take hold of that which Christ Jesus took hold of me. Brothers, I do not consider myself yet to have taken hold of it. But one thing I do: Forgetting what is behind and straining toward what is ahead. I press on toward the goal to win the prize for which God has called me heavenward in Christ Jesus" (Philippians 3:12–14).*

The greatest thing about destiny is that your destiny never ends, it keeps unfolding before you. You may accomplish a portion of what God has planned for you, but He will surprise you with new promises for your future that He has in store for you. Press on toward the goal of oneness with Him and you will find a deep well of gifts waiting to be received.

You are the treasure that God longs for. His reward is to have more and more of your heart and life devoted to Him, to have more of your mind and body consecrated to Him. He wants to have more of you! This is His great passion, this is His goal, and this is destiny's purpose.

Enjoy the journey of experiencing your destiny in God. Enjoy all aspects of the journey, even the little things. For one day you may look back across your life and realize that they were the most notable things you were privileged to experience.

Enjoy your journey with God! Press on . . .

[1.] *destiny.* Webster's Seventh New Collegiate Dictionary
Copyright 1971 G. & C. Merriam Co.

IN CONCLUSION

*I*t is my prayer that this book has breathed life into your dreams, given you direction, and maybe even done a little spiritual surgery on your heart. Reread it as many times as you need to. You may find the Lord will continue to give you new revelation as you do.

It is my sincere desire for you to be blessed and walk in the fullness of not only your destiny but also the richness of Christ Himself. Remember, Christ revealed through you is the hope of all heaven. Your goal is to know Him. You are the light by which the world finds its Savior . . . so let Jesus shine through you!

In His love,

Victoria

CONFERENCE INFORMATION

If you would like to invite Victoria
to speak at your church or conference,
you may do so by using the information
provided on the next page.

Thank you and God bless!

FREE EMAIL NEWSLETTER

Victoria sends out a free newsletter via email.
The newsletter includes:

•Anointed Articles

•Prayer Alerts

•Special Announcements

•Special Offers

To sign up for our free email newsletter:

VISIT OUR WEBSITE
www.boyson.org

To Place an Order for

The Birth of
Your Destiny

by
Victoria Boyson

Visit our website:
www.boyson.org

Write to us:
Victoria Boyson, Inc.
P.O. Box 10441
Cedar Rapids, IA 52410

Call our order line:
1-319-365-9570

Fax us:
1-319-365-9570

Email us:
info@boyson.org

Contact us about Quantity Discounts!

Be sure and ask your
favorite local Christian bookstore to stock

The Birth of
Your Destiny

by Victoria Boyson